Jungle R

Alexander Bar ... *Times* and *Daily Tele* ...

During the Se ... AF. He has flown all ... n Kane books and has received full co ... his research into military planes and equipment.

Also by Alexander Barrie
in the Jonathan Kane Series in Piccolo

Fly for Three Lives
Operation Midnight
Let Them All Starve

Alexander Barrie

Jungle Run

cover illustration by C. L. Doughty
text illustrations by Paul Wright

Piccolo Pan Books

First published 1977 by Frederick Muller Ltd
This abridged edition published 1978 by Pan Books Ltd,
Cavaye Place, London SW10 9PG

ISBN 0 330 25347 6
Printed and bound in Great Britain by
Richard Clay (The Chaucer Press) Ltd, Bungay, Suffolk

For Tom, my brother

I have to thank my family again for help with this book, especially my wife and younger son, Giles, who typed part of the manuscript. My thanks, also, to John Willis of Fairflight Charters Ltd, and to David Rafique and Valerie Kirwan for many kindnesses. Also to Daniel Knox.

Contents

More about Jonno

Jonathan Kane was seven years old, and shopping with his mother, when he saw a book with the title *How an Aeroplane Flies*. It was on a bookshop counter. He stared at the cover for a while, then looked at some pages, and then plagued his mother into buying it. 'You'll never understand that,' she grumbled at the time. She was wrong. With a little help, he mastered the theory of flight – and his life changed. If an aircraft flew over the house, Jonno would be out through the back door to spot it. At every chance he went to airports to watch the aircraft on the ground and in the air. He talked, thought and slept aeroplanes.

By the age of nine he could identify hundreds of civilian and military planes, often when they were flying high; which is not the easiest of things to do. For his tenth birthday his parents bought him a subscription to a flying magazine, written for adult, licence-holding pilots. By twelve, he had had a number of joy-rides in aircraft, including a memorable trip in an open-cockpit bi-plane, the Stampe.

At thirteen he played his master-stroke by persuading Perry Langhorne, owner of the struggling Western Aircharters Company, of Lonehead Field, to let him help out. He washed the aircraft, taxied them, and before long (predictably) flew them. Jonno became friendly with the Lonehead crew of three – Perry, his girlfriend Roz, and the knock-about flying instructor, Charlie Thompson. The friendship with Charlie was particularly strong.

1 Business in Burma

The wide, open smile on Jonathan Kane's face faded. 'Aren't I going then? Is that it?'

Perry looked back at him awkwardly. 'Jeeze, Jonno,' he said, the drawled voice diminishing to a murmur. 'See ... Jeeze, this time it's difficult. We'd love to have you along. Really.'

'Then take me,' urged Jonathan. 'Please Perry. Take me. I mean I do go most places, and I'm often useful, and I'm supposed to be one of the team. If I go with you I just bet something happens and you'll be glad I'm there and sorry if I'm not.'

'Sure, absolutely right, we're always glad to have you along, Jonno, useful or not, you know that – and yeah, you are useful and you are one of the team, hell yes. But, see, it costs a lot of dough to fly a commercial jet to Rangoon. It's a long, long, long, long way. It's, see, it's a matter of, well, I don't know how we can raise the pesetas.' Peregrene Langhorne, owner and chief pilot of the struggling Western Aircharters Company, looked round at the others, the customary blandness gone, and raised his lean brown hands in a spreading gesture of perplexity. 'What we going to do about Jonno?' he asked. 'Somebody say something if it's only "yahoo".'

They were in the untidy sitting room of Perry's rambling, one-time farm-house at Lonehead Field. Jonathan, miserable, stood near the door, his small red suitcase on the floor beside him. He'd arrived full of 13-year-old bounce and happiness five minutes or so earlier, at the start of the Easter break from school. These days he spent as much of every holiday as he could at Lonehead helping with the aircraft. He washed them, polished windows, brushed carpets, refuelled and taxied them to and fro by himself, which Perry had come to trust him enough to do.

Taxiing – now that *was* something, especially taxiing Western Air's star aircraft, the Aztec D, call sign Golf Alpha X-ray India Victor, often just India Victor.

Easing the brakes off in the beautifully fitted-out cockpit of India Victor; hearing the melodious roar as the twin Lycoming's 540s brought their combined 500 horsepower into action; feeling the aircraft start to roll and to know it was under the sole command of Captain Jonathan Kane – yes, that was truly something; an embodiment of joy.

Then there was the real business of flying. Jonathan did a lot of that, flying with Perry or Charlie Thompson – or sometimes with members of the little Mid Country Flying Club to whom Charlie was chief instructor. And when Jonno went flying, he really flew. With an inflatable cushion under his bottom and another behind his back, he could reach the controls; all of which he handled skilfully. Between them, Perry and Charlie had made sure he was a good pilot and a safe one. He often took the controls from the right hand, co-pilot's seat in the Aztec while Perry or Charlie sneaked a rest in the left. When he took over he did it all, steering an accurate course, keeping his height and airspeed dead on, tuning the nav aids in for himself, making the radio calls – and not only making them, but making them the way they should be made: clearly, quickly and with courtesy. 'Remember,' Charlie had once said, 'we're very polite in aviation circles.' The boy had understood and found this aspect, the little pleasantries, oddly agreeable. Those

'Good mornings' and 'Thank yous' civilized the remoteness of radio contact. To be smashing your way through solid grey cloud, feeling the loneliness of flying blind, and then to have someone wish you 'Good morning', someone miles away and thousands of feet below, that was always a strangely comforting moment.

But it wasn't solely cross-country flying at Lonehead. They had an ageing aerobatic Beagle Pup on the field which Charlie and Jonno used to fly together just for fun. Jonathan's own repertoire was limited to the loop, spin and barrel roll, but they would be moving on to the rest of it soon. Charlie, of course, could do anything from an all-the-way-round bunt to a triple snap roll. That is, if the aircraft could, and not many of today's 'dollied up tinware' (Charlie's expression) could.

Jonno often wondered quite a bit about his own attitude to the stomach-churning thrill of aerobatics. The truth was they scared him, yet in a subtle mix of emotions, delighted him too. When Charlie grinned through his wild red moustache and said, 'Come on, Captain, let's put the Pup on its back,' his heart would start a hammer-action he'd come to know well, so well, good grief but so well! His young, round face would signal the strain – a fractional set of mouth and eyes – and Charlie, noticing, would nudge him with a hefty elbow and maybe say, 'Race you to the aircraft,' and they'd be away together pounding across the grass. Jonno would do the take-off and climb-out from the circuit which kept him quietly busy. But, as they slammed into each aerobatic, right at the beginning, there would be more of the fear thing, followed half-way through by a vast, relaxed enjoyment. This pure pleasure, excitement without fear, would begin when the ground was where the sky should be as they came soaring inverted over the top of a loop;

or as the spin-rate began to slow from the full opposite rudder and stick forward recovery drill – and the blurred green splodge you were tumbling towards turned into trees and fields. This was the pure pleasure of having faced a challenge of nerve and skill and arriving at the moment when you knew you were the winner.

Then, the manoeuvre completed, came the soft glow of achievement, quiet but prolonged in the tranquillity of straight and level flight while they talked, reconstructing the sequence, probing into little errors of speed or direction in the endless effort to find perfection. And, after that, the next sky-swoop; more tension, relief and self-fulfilment.

And when the flight was finished, as they strolled towards the tower, came the last reward – that feeling of well-being, a great envelopment that seemed to touch every cell of mind and body. Jonno walked taller, looked at the world through more confident eyes. 'I did okay then, Charlie?'

'Yessir, fine, fine. Bit fast coming out of the loops at times, pull it in a little tighter over the tops there – but not bad at all. You're a pilot, Captain. How d'you feel?'

'Okay, thanks.'

That was a point, too. Just at first, in the early trips, he'd had his stomach to battle with, once at least reckoning he'd been within a minute of bringing his breakfast up. Not now; there was nothing physical to worry about in half an hour or more of zooming, fluttering, flicking and pulling G.

In the tower, a big-windowed room set in the hangar roof, Roz – Rosemary-Anne Hart, Perry's girl and generalissimo of flying control – would greet them, often with coffee or coke. 'That looked pretty good, Jonno. I could see you in the distance.' The boy would smile, shrug, mutter a sentence of thanks and sit by the window to sip his drink, watch for action in Lonehead's circuit and perhaps man the radio for a while.

These were typical scenes. All this, the whole fascinating business of aviation, and the friendships that were part of it, were what Jonathan reckoned he mainly lived for. But now, this bleak day, he'd turned up to find the three of them – even Charlie – were shoving off without him. Jonathan moved his sharp brown eyes, uncharacteristically clouded for the moment, from Perry to Charlie. The stare had power and accusation behind it.

Charlie sat on the edge of the window-sill at the far end of the room, right knee clamped in his big hands, right foot off the ground and wriggling with unease. 'For crying out loud, Jonno,' he said. 'Come in! Don't stand by the door like a miniature Moses.'

Jonathan came in and sat down in a sagging armchair on Charlie's left and about opposite Roz, who was sitting in a similar but better chair on the other side of a low white coffee table. She looked as delectable as ever, long blonde hair, slender figure and dancing smile all stunningly set off by a vivid yellow jacket and matching trousers. 'Hi, Jonno,' she said eagerly, turning towards him. 'It's good to see you. How've you been these last few weeks?'

'Okay, I suppose.'

Charlie turned his head, with the reddish hair and colour-matched moustache all in its routine disarray, and stared at Perry – who still stood to the side of the door defensively.

'It's only money,' he said. 'Sell something.'

'Hmm.' Perry scratched the underside of his chin and took a lingering look at the ceiling. 'Hmm. Mr Thompson says "Sell something" – brilliant, brilliant, except for one thing. He doesn't say what. Anyway, you know, it's as late as hell but maybe we don't need money. Maybe Clyne will pay. How about this?' He tore a slip off a message pad and wrote,

REQUIRE FURTHER MEMBER OF CREW STOP YOUR OKAY ASSUMED STOP FLYING WITH US FLIGHT BA EIGHT FIVE ZERO FRIDAY LANGHORNE.

Charlie studied the words. 'Great,' he said. 'Send that. Send it now.'

'Okay,' Perry turned to Roz. 'Phone this cable for me, Roz – you little old bit of warmed up cherry pie. Top rate, first class, express delivery, immediate – all that.' He handed her the piece of paper.

Indignation, more put on than real, flickered across Roz's face. 'Some men were born lazy,' she said. 'Warmed up cherry pie? And old? You certainly say the sweetest things, Perry. Jonno, here, you send the thing. Well, never mind, I'll do it.' She had noticed the change that was flooding over Jonathan and didn't want to spoil it for him.

The frown was gone and the smile was back – showing even white teeth; and then there were the eyes, they looked the way they normally did, in full sparkle again, sidelines of tension gone. Perry came over and held out his hand. 'Shake, Jonno,' he said. 'I'm really glad you're coming.' He jerked his left thumb towards Charlie. 'If you think he's the beauty and I'm the beast in all this, it isn't actually quite like that. See, if we'd known you were coming we'd have negotiated. We thought you had a boys' camp or something, so we just didn't expect you. And it was old Mr Beautiful, there, who gave out the information.'

Jonno scrambled to his feet and shook hands. 'Thanks, Perry, thanks. No, but it wasn't Charlie's fault – there *was* to be a camp. I didn't want to go but my dad said just this once I must. Then Mr Green – he was taking us – broke his leg. Fantastic luck. I phoned by the way, left a message with ...' He faltered through the last few words seeing more awkwardness ahead.

'You did?' said Perry dangerously. 'That means you spoke to Gerry. Right? Don't bother to answer. There must be some way we can teach that guy to write things down. He's gonna lose us something big before he's through. Makes me mad.'

'He's ... he's a super mechanic. And he *means* to remember, I think he just kind of finds it hard.'

'Anyway,' said Roz soothingly, 'it's turned out all right, Jonno, I'm glad you're coming, too. Really glad. The full team.'

'Thanks, Roz.'

'I'll send the cable, then you call your mum. Clear it with her.'

'Yes, I'll phone. It'll be okay with them.'

'And there's something else. You're gonna need a visa – Charlie will have to whip you down to London – to sort that out at the Burmese embassy. I'd better call them first to get things moving.'

Charlie's large form, heavy without being fat, came ambling across the room now. 'That seems to have turned out rather well, Captain Kane,' he said. 'And, as it happens, *I'm* glad you're coming along, too.'

'I know, Charlie.' Then suddenly thinking that maybe he had sounded smug, 'What I mean is, thanks.'

Charlie shook his head sideways. 'You had it right – what you mean is, you *know*. And thanks are not required. My turn to shake hands?'

'You bet.' Charlie had the big hands that went with a large-boned man; big but by no means clumsy. He proved that with every flight as he tuned to the aircraft's behaviour through his fingertips, sensing every change in performance or attitude and every tremor of the airframe, then answering with sensitive corrections he was barely aware of making. Jonathan put his slight hand into Charlie's big one, looked up at the light blue eyes, sprouting moustache and canyon-like grin, and smiled again.

Roz got up, making her way to the telephone. 'Do you want to put your bag upstairs now, Jonno?' she asked. 'We fly out on Friday, so you've got a couple of nights to kick about here. Your usual five-star attic room. Bit cramped, isn't it? I sometimes wonder if you overheat up there.'

'No. It's a great room. I can see most of the field from there and miles of countryside.'

Charlie picked up his bag. 'Come on,' he said. 'Let's get the show organized.'

Upstairs, Jonathan threw his pyjamas, handkerchiefs, toothbrush, spare shirts, socks and underpants, and a pair of mid-blue shorts in a random heap on the bed. 'Nice bit of unpacking, that,' murmured Charlie drily, and wandered over to look through the little south facing window.

Jonno sprawled face down on the bed, left arm trailing onto the floor. 'It's really good to be back,' he said. 'That was awful down there. I mean being left behind.'

'You'd never be left behind – you know that.'

A pause followed, and then, 'Charlie – what's the big trip supposed to be for? Where's Rangoon, that place Perry was blabbing on about – the cost of getting there and everything?'

Charlie twisted round to look at him. 'Don't they teach you kids anything at school these days?'

'No.'

'Rangoon is the capital of Burma, and Burma is, ah, it's, you go to India and sort of turn left. And I'll tell you something else, Jonno. At this time of year Rangoon is hot. Oh boy, hot.'

Another pause while Jonathan pondered and Charlie waited, idly looking down at his feet.

'Burma's mostly jungle, isn't it?'

'Mostly.'

'Snakes.'

'Right. Snakes, monkeys, elephants, bugs – they're all there.'

'Tigers?'

'Must be. Real man-eaters I expect. Boy-eaters, too.'

'Very funny. So what are we going to do in Burma, and who's Clyne?'

Charlie shrugged. 'It's all a bit vague. Clyne is some kind of doctor – not the kind who tells you to take an Aspro for your headache, but one of those egg-heads. Doctor of Science I think. He's an expert in farming rough land and he's helping the Burmese government. They've got erosion problems, if you know what that means.'

'No.'

'Didn't think you would. It means the topsoil's blowing away, and that's the good stuff for growing things. Clyne's got some airlifting problem we're supposed to help with. That's all we know. Came up very suddenly. Just as well because business has been really bad here just recently – when poor old Perry does his figures it's best to keep out of the way for a while. Profits down, costs up – all that. Then this character cables and it's all go-go-go. Perry knew him years ago.'

'Perry seems to know *everybody*.'

'That's true. He's certainly been around a bit. International citizen, remember, that's what he calls himself.'

'He's American though, really. He's still got a drawly American voice.'

'So? You can be American international, French international, English international, anything international. It's just a matter of outlook. Come on – get off that bed.'

Downstairs they found the house empty, and strolled out onto the field – a pleasant, fresh-smelling day in spring; bright, cloudy with a 10 to 15 knot breeze from the south-west filling the yellow windsock.

'How's India Victor?' asked Jonathan, looking across at the Aztec D pointed nose to wind and parked well clear of the grass runway in use, two-two, on one-one.

'Meaning you want to have a look!'

'Of course.'

'Go on then.'

'Er, d'you think I could start her up?'

Charlie groped about in his hip pocket and produced the keys. 'Who's a bore?' he said. 'And *don't* forget your pre-start checks. And don't burn up too much fuel. And there are all the other don'ts I can't think of right now – don't do any of them.'

'Thanks.' Jonathan took the keys and was just beginning to run joyfully towards the aircraft when Roz called from an open window in the hangar roof 'tower'.

'Hey, you two,' she yelled. 'Come up here, please. You've got to go to the embassy right away.'

Jonathan stopped, turned, scowled and walked slowly back to Charlie. 'Just my flipping luck,' he said. They headed for the hangar entrance, then clambered up the long flight of stairs to the roof where Roz was waiting.

'I've sent the cable to Clyne,' she said. 'And I've had a chat with the cultural attaché at the embassy. He says if you get down there today he'll have the papers cleared by Thursday. It's just gone twelve – get moving now and you should be there by four, easily. Take Perry's car. I've asked him.'

Perry's car was a Mark 3 MG Midget a trifle out of tune. As they reached the little car Jonathan said, 'I'll drive as far as the entrance – I hope the cushion's in the back.' Laboriously, Charlie heaved his bulk into the passenger's seat.

'Funny, but I thought you might,' he said, as Jonathan stuffed the cushion into place behind his back and started up.

They stopped for cheeseburgers and coffee on the way, found the embassy, filled in forms – the usual full name, sex, date of birth, address, purpose of visit nonsense – then headed out of town, trapped now in the peak of the city's rush hour. 'Blimey, I'm glad I don't live here,' muttered Jonathan as they sat locked in lane two of a five lane phalanx of motionless traffic.

'Yeah, me too. Let's hear you run through the pre-flight checks. T T M P – come on.'

'Oh blimey – do I have to?'

'Yeah.'

'Er, Trim for take-off, Throttle friction nut right, Mixture rich and cold carburettor air, Pitch fine, Pitot uncovered, Fuel okay and booster pump on, Flaps set, Gyros and Gauges functioning, Hatches closed and Harness tight. Whew!'

'And the mnemonic?'

'The ...? Oh yes, that stupid word again. T T M P P F F G G H H.'

'Top marks, Captain. For that we'll think of several reasons why India Victor has to be taxied around the field in the morning.'

Jonathan turned on the full smile, and they battled on northwards. As the long minutes passed, Charlie's temper deteriorated. He switched lanes twice and got hooted at once. 'Listen to that silly clod,' he snarled, moustache sticking out like a porcupine's quills. 'Who the hell does he think he's honking at?'

'Well, you're not a very good driver, you know,' said Jonathan.

Charlie turned to glower at him. 'Thanks,' he said. 'Remarks like that really help.'

After what seemed like a month they reached the motorway and got going well, cruising at seventy, more or less without interruption. Timing it neatly, about three miles before a service area, Jonno announced he was hungry again, and they pulled off the road and went in to eat. With sausages, chips, beans and a coke inside him, he became conversational. 'Why can't we fly ourselves to Rangoon in India Victor? We've done long trips before.'

'Several reasons. First, that's what Clyne wants. He's fixed the tickets, and it's a lot cheaper that way. Second, India Victor is up for a new C of A* and, apart from the rest, her propellers are due for an overhaul. Will that do for starters?'

Jonathan ran his right first finger round the rim of the plate. 'It's a pity, though, isn't it Charlie? Flying out in a jet isn't much fun. We'll just be ordinary passengers. Boring. But we'll be doing some proper flying out in Burma I take it, won't we?'

'I reckon so. They've got a Dove out there. You know the Dove?'

'Yes. An old twin.'

'That's it – and a big chunk of aeroplane. You actually seem to have stopped eating, let's go.'

They finished the journey in darkness and for the last hour or more Jonno slept, head hard down on his chest, hands limp and cupped, resting on his lap.

Inside the house they found Roz and Perry playing snooker. 'Thank God you've come,' said Roz. 'I hate this game and I can't play it – you take my cue.'

'Hell's teeth, we've just got in,' complained Charlie. But he took the cue and sized up the lie of the balls on the table. Roz looked happier.

'Was everything all right?' she went on.

'Yep. Fine. The Captain's tired, though, and he's going to bed.'

In the morning Charlie woke him by lifting the end of the bed and shaking it rapidly up and down. 'C'mon, c'mon,' he said loudly, as Jonathan opened a sleepy eye. 'We've got to fly India Victor to Oxford – Kidlington

* C of A means Certificate of Airworthiness.

Airport. Ten minutes to take off, you and me, so don't hang about.'

Jonathan scrambled out of bed. 'You mean now?' he asked. 'We're going right now?'

'Yessir. Just as fast as you can climb into your clothes and swallow a bit of breakfast.'

Jonno was downstairs in at most, three minutes; unwashed of course since he knew it wouldn't show. He found Perry munching through a breakfast of cereal and chopped banana. 'Hi there,' said Perry. 'You okay? Grab some breakfast – Roz says that's yours on the hotplate. Then we hit the trail.'

'Are you coming too?' He picked up a plate of eggs (two), bacon and fried bread, and sat down beside Perry.

'You and Charlie fly the Aztec, I pick you up in the Pup. So you're the one in a hurry, and *you're* in a hurry because Charlie is – don't ask me why, he's just feeling that way. He's already out there at the aircraft doing his DI.'

'Blimey!' Jonathan began to cram the breakfast into his mouth at enormous speed but still spluttered through a question. 'Are we leaving India Victor there?'

'Right. She goes to Kidlington while we go to Burma. She's done going on twelve hundred hours – just about out of time, see? We'll drop her off at CSE for overhaul and a new airworthiness certificate. Those C of A's are goddam expensive.' Perry's munch-rate slowed down at the thought.

Clutching his cushions, Jonno raced across the grass to the silent Aztec. Charlie was inside so he must have finished the DI – the routine daily inspection. Jonathan clambered onto the wing, opened the door and dropped into the vacant right hand seat. Charlie helped ram the cushions into position. 'Let's go flying,' he said laconically. A calmer mood had taken over.

'Me?'

'You. You're captain.'

'Okay, great.' The start-up was quick, Captain Kane running nimbly through the cockpit movements. Brakes on, master switch, fuel cock, booster pumps, pitch controls to fine, mixture rich, six brisk forward and back priming strokes of the left throttle, a quick look round outside the aircraft, then starter switch – press left. The port propeller began a jerky rotation, and a moment later the big Lycoming fired and spun loudly at fifteen hundred rpm, warming up. Seconds later the starboard engine was running too.

He went briskly through the rest of the vital pre-flight actions, Charlie nodding occasionally with approval as he watched the young hands flit from control to control, sequences correct and movements adroitly and confidently made. Jonno adjusted the boom microphone an inch ahead of his mouth and pressed the transmit button. 'Lonehead. India Victor. Ready to line up and take off, for Kidlington.'

As usual, Roz was in the tower. 'India Victor,' she said briskly. 'Take off at your discretion. QNH one-zero-one-eight.'

Jonathan acknowledged. 'One-zero-one-eight. India Victor.' He turned to Charlie with arched eyebrows – a wordless question replied to with a wordless answer, a pushing forward gesture of both hands. Jonathan understood, released the brakes and the aircraft rolled towards two-two rocking gently on the uneven grass, turned into wind (heavy right rudder for this, Jonno's leg fully extended and the cushions proving their value) and lined up. He took two deep breaths, glanced at Charlie for reassurance, then with his left hand pushed the throttles smoothly forward. The twin Lycomings roared up to take-off power and India Victor, flagship of Western Air-charters, accelerated rapidly down the long grass strip. A gentle back-pull on the ram's horn control stick eased the load off the drubbing nosewheel and, soon after that, the whole aircraft lifted just clear skimming the tops of the grass. The gap between grass and gear widened; they were safely airborne. Jonathan touched the toe-brakes to check the fast-spinning wheels, selected gear up, flashed over the boundary hedge and settled to the climb at 105 knots. At 200 feet he brought the flaps in and finally left the circuit in a slow climbing turn onto a first course of one-seven-zero en route for Kidlington.

Captain Kane did the whole job, beacon-hopped to Kidlington, identified the field, selected the radio frequency, called for permission to join the circuit and land, and came in without any need for help from Charlie. The landing itself was a trifle disappointing; on the heavy side and further down the field than he intended, but safe. He swore a bit as he taxied towards the parking area and banged the side of his head with his hand. But Charlie was comforting. 'I've seen pilots with a thousand hours come in heavier than that,' he said. 'And you've never landed here before. Relax, Jonno, relax.' He patted the boy twice lightly on the knee. 'You did a hell of a good job, and you did it all alone.'

They wandered about for half an hour or so until Perry taxied over in the Beagle Pup, then spent a full two hours arranging the overhaul for India Victor. For the flight home to Lonehead, Perry and Charlie took the front seats. Perry, looking gloomy (an estimate of cost was burning through his pocket) did the flying – his usual polished, immaculate performance that a state of mind, however low, could never affect. Jonno felt sad too, sitting idly in the back; sad at being parted from the Aztec –

and the fact that it was for a good cause, an essential cause, didn't do much to help.

Still, there would be – should be – the Dove to fly before long – and over the harsh terrain of Burma. He thought about that for a while and felt gradually nervous which, on the whole, was a better way to feel than sad. It would be nice to get on with it. Roll on Friday.

2 Clyne's strange family

They arrived in the departure lounge of Terminal 3, London Airport, at about twelve-thirty (midday-plus), and were already tired. It had been an early start and a tedious journey by train, subway and airport bus. All four of them were there – Perry, Charlie, Roz and Jonathan, and they reacted in character. Perry seemed outwardly relaxed but had gone quieter than was normal even for him; Charlie was gruff and ready for a row with anyone; Roz closed her eyes for a moment at times but seemed otherwise unaffected; Jonno wore a practised air of boredom which he put aside occasionally – like once when Roz bought him an ice-cream, and again when a young woman's bag fell from a moving trolley and scattered intimate clothing on the floor.

They had checked in for Flight BA 850, departing 1400 hours, destination Rangoon with short stopovers at Muscat and Calcutta. There had been no snags at the desk – tickets good, papers in order. Now it was just stand or sit about, and wait, and wait.

'Not exactly VIPs – are we?' muttered Charlie, mainly to Perry. 'Trains and economy class and all that. How the hell can there be so many people on the move all the time?' Perry shrugged and drifted away to look at duty free goods on display. Jonathan joined him examining watches temptingly set out, all glitter, glamour and plush. The prices were astounding.

'Blimey,' said Jonathan. 'Look at that! I thought duty free things were meant to be cheap.'

'Yeah,' said Perry. 'That's the myth. Just another great government con.'

At last the announcement came. 'Calling passengers for Flight BA 850, Muscat, Calcutta and Rangoon. Leave by gate four please, and have your boarding passes ready. Flight BA 850, gate four.'

Despite the crowd in the departure lounge, Flight 850 turned out to be underbooked. They were able to sit in pairs, Perry and Roz, then behind them, Charlie and Jonno, each pair with a three-seat row to share. Charlie pushed Jonno through to the window position. 'Enjoy the view while you can,' he said. 'You won't see a lot at forty thousand feet.' The stewardess converted the vacant chairs into tables and tidied the hand baggage away in overhead lockers.

'Anyway, it's comfortable,' remarked Jonathan, reaching up for the ventilation control. 'Really good.'

'Just as well. We've got twelve hours to sit here. Get your seatbelt properly tight – look at it.'

The doors shut and immediately the Rolls-Royce Conways started up. Jonathan listened to the turbofan-whine coming agreeably through the insulation of the fuselage and noticed the airframe quiver as they waited to roll. 'Boy, there's some power there,' he said.

'Yeah.'

Then the aircraft began its long taxi to the holding point. 'Boy,' said Jonathan, 'these jets taxi fast.'

'Yeah.'

The take-off run had him gripping the armrests and gazing through the porthole-type windows as the runway began to disappear behind them in a blur of skidmarks, lights and tarmac. 'Fantastic acceleration,' he said loudly. Then came rotation – tail down and nose up high. He turned quickly to Charlie. 'Blimey,' he said, 'look at that. We could stall!'

'Yeah.'

'What?'

'We won't. You've done too much flying with props, haven't you chief? All jets have this sort of climb angle.' He laughed. 'And who was it said it would all be so boring? I think you're scared.'

'I am *not*.'

'Don't worry about it – it's people who know, you know, who sometimes are.'

'I'm not scared, you dimmo.'

'Okay, okay.'

They played pokerdice, had drinks and later a three-course meal and, in the early evening, a smiling stewardess came over to settle Jonathan down for a sleep. She put his chair into maximum recline and gently spread a blanket over him. The timing was good. He felt ready to sleep, turned his head to the left and slowly closed his eyes.

Charlie leaned over him. 'I don't seem to be getting the tuck-in treatment like that,' he said – and paused. 'Not even a "good night" – just a blooming blanket stuck in my hand.' No answer. Out already, God that was quick. He studied the young sleeping face for a while, then Charlie, too, settled down for a snooze. Roz looked over the top of her chair a little later to check that all was well and saw them both asleep.

'They're a funny pair,' she said, laughing, to Perry.

'Let's join the club and go to sleep,' mumbled Perry through a half-checked yawn. 'It's a long, long road ahead.'

'Let's do that.' They tilted their seats back, Roz took

Perry's hand in hers and they nodded off too, as the big VC 10 hammered south-eastwards at 550 miles an hour, 38,000 feet.

Flight 850 came in to Rangoon Airport on schedule at nine-forty in the morning, local time. The passengers, about fifty of them at this tail end of the journey, straggled across the already warm tarmac to customs and immigration, filled in more forms, showed passports and visas and opened bags, then filed into the outer area of the airport building. As Perry led his group through a swing door, he gave a quick, soft shout. 'There's Clyne!' At the same moment Clyne saw Peregrene, and the two approached each other and shook hands with obvious warmth. 'It's been a long time, Walt,' said Perry.

'Right. Too long. But you're looking good.'

'And you. Say, I'd like you to meet the mob. Walt, this is Roz.'

'Good to know you, Roz. Now, let's get this right – are you Perry's...?'

'Not yet,' said Roz quickly sensing the finish of the question. 'But I'll get him someday.' She laughed, and Clyne grinned appreciatively, then took her by the arm.

'Be sure he's worth it,' he said. 'Remember I know the fella.'

Perry carried blandly on with the introduction. 'This hairy one is Charles Thompson, sort of my partner in the charter business. Charlie, meet Walter Clyne.' The two shook hands and nodded cordially.

'And this is, ah, the extra member of the crew we wired about, Jonathan Kane, pilot, washer-down and runner of errands – in short, a key man.'

Clyne stretched out a hand for Jonno's. 'A pleasure to meet you, Jonathan,' he said, and clearly meant it. 'I bet you're a useful guy to have around.' Jonno went momentarily pink about the face and muttered a 'thank you'.

'So that's the complete outfit, eh? Now I want you to meet a friend of mine,' said Clyne, looking round. 'Joe – come on over here.' He beckoned to a tall, leanly built man with hair that seemed to belong to somebody else – almost white hair, quite long, on a youngish-looking face.

The man moved towards them. He came warily, unsmiling, showing a just detectable limp affecting his right leg or foot. His face, though sharply intelligent, had pronounced peculiarities. The lips were compressed – thin, straight and challenging. More noticeable and disconcerting were the eyes, grey eyes of lustreless tone set unusually deep in his face. They moved with furtive quickness. They glanced, darted and judged, but judged without themselves pausing to be judged; they were eyes in retreat, of no trust, eyes that fled from the eyes of others, that hinted at secrets, that gave nothing away, that sought no involvement. And yet, despite all that, despite the obvious oddness of this approaching face, it did have an appeal and a compelling interest – this was by no means the face of an ordinary man.

'Roz,' Clyne continued, still the soul of cordiality, 'meet Joe Bergman. Joe, meet – listen, I should have more of a name than Roz to work on.'

'Rosemary-Anne Hart,' said Roz quickly. 'That's the whole story – but Roz is good enough. Hullo, Joe.' Bergman kept his hands wedged in his pockets but nodded.

'And here we have the rest of the gang,' added Clyne, speeding up the ceremonial. 'That's Perry, that's Charles and that's Jonathan.'

'Huh-huh,' said Bergman.

Charlie had folded his arms across his considerable chest and was watching Bergman candidly. 'I'm Charlie,' he said. 'Negative Charles. And this is Jonno.' He pointed to the boy. 'He's Jonno, Jon, Captain Kane, sir or you-there as the case may be.'

'Okay, I'm with all that,' said Bergman. 'What next, Walt?'

'The Strand Hotel next. Look, Perry, you've arrived at the hot season. I hope you knew that.'

'Sure, we knew.'

'We did?' queried Roz. 'How hot is hot, Walt?'

'When it's hot in Rangoon it's *really* hot. And humid. You get the whole works. I reckon you're all tired, or you surely soon will be, so I've figured out a little plan. We take a cab down to the Strand Hotel – it's got a sort of steam driven air conditioner which helps. You all freshen up there and have a rest while Joe and I go about some business. We've got a few thousand day-old chicks to collect – but I'll go into that kind of detail later. Then we meet around three at the hotel for lunch. A little late, I guess, by western standards. You can have a look around the city if you want to, before or after, only remember it's going to be as hot as Hades. Anyhow, I've booked us in for the night, see, then we leave early in the morning for the farm in Shan State. We'll fly out in the Dove.'

'The chicks and us, eh?' said Perry.

'Right. Does that sound okay?'

'Just great, great.' The rest of them nodded agreement.

'Okay. Joe, let's find a cab.'

Bergman came back with a battered Honda and smiling Burmese driver. Six of them, plus driver, plus baggage – 'Hey,' muttered Jonno to Charlie, 'we can't all get in that!' But after a sweaty struggle they did. The bags were stacked high like Pisa's leaning tower on the roof. Perry sat in front with Roz on his knees – and they were by far the best off. Bergman, Clyne and Charlie squeezed themselves onto the back seat, Bergman in centre place, then hauled Jonno inside and pushed him down on their feet, jammed in by a cliff-face of knees against the back of the front seats. Despite the gross overloading, the car set off down the thinly tarmaced road at high speed; swaying, thumping and jarring.

Jonathan, still wearing his jeans and jacket, was soaked in his own sweatbath from the start. 'I think I'm going to be sick,' he said faintly.

A bus screamed past them going the other way flat-out in what seemed to be an abnormally low gear. 'My God, this is murder!' said Charlie. 'We can't leave the kid down there.'

'It's just a few miles,' said Clyne mildly. 'We must all stick it out.'

The thumping and jarring went on. 'How's the view, Captain?' asked Charlie in a hopeless attempt at humour. 'It's great fun here – I'll keep you informed.' Jonathan didn't answer and Charlie took a careful look at him, then reached forward, put his strong hands under the boy's arms and heaved.

The disturbance angered Bergman. 'What the hell are you trying to do?' he asked.

'I'm getting this kid off the floor,' snarled Charlie. 'I'm getting him where he can breathe – that's what I'm doing.' He hauled upward again. Now Jonathan's shoulders and back were on Charlie's lap, his knees in Bergman's face and his shoes somewhere near Clyne's chest and shoulder. Bergman prised the knees clear of his mouth, and swore.

'Easy everyone,' said Clyne. 'Easy, easy.' Charlie put a wet arm under Jonathan's head, then re-positioned it to cradle his neck.

'I reckon that's better,' he said. 'Yes?'

'Yes,' gulped Jonathan.

Then Clyne jerked as a foot caught him a sudden blow on the lips. 'Get his feet over the seat back,' he said, feeling and guarding his mouth. 'To the left of Perry, there – maybe one on each side.'

'Stick it out, Walt,' said Charlie. 'It's just a few miles. Remember?'

It was actually nine, nine punishing miles to the hotel, nine miles in a rolling, bouncing, baking oven – a very long mileage indeed.

They arrived at last and tottered into the comparative coolness of the Strand Hotel. Jonathan was making his way through the lobby when he stopped abruptly and squawked. 'Lizards!' he said.

Clyne, beside him, nodded and grinned. 'Geckos,' he said. 'Friendly little fellas. They make a clicking sound – but they won't hurt you. Honest. And they eat the mosquitoes.'

Perry and Roz had bedrooms to themselves. Clyne shared with Bergman, and Charlie with Jonno. As Clyne had proposed, the Lonehead four went off for a rest, free of all engagements until three. 'You know what we're going to do?' said Charlie as soon as he and Jonathan had found their way to their room. 'We're going to use that.' He pointed to a shower closet. 'We're going to have a long, cold, wet, bea-utiful shower. You first. Don't use all the water.'

Jonathan stripped, then stood for a full ten minutes in the cascade of cold water, stood until he was chilled, enjoying the chill and the sense of sanctuary. Then he came out and dried off while Charlie stepped in and shuddered and grunted with noisy pleasure. Jonno pulled his shorts on and flopped on a bed well back from the window. 'You sound like a rhino,' he called.

'Aaah,' answered Charlie. 'Brrr-r.' He came out at last, hair and moustache streaming and looked over at the comfortably sprawled boy. 'I see,' he said. 'I get the hot one. Thanks.'

Charlie zipped up his trousers, closed the slatted shutters which dimmed out the sun, then he, too, flopped on the bed. 'I hope you never come as close to a sticky end in an aircraft as you did in that taxi,' he said. 'The driver was screwy.'

'You're telling me. It was awful, really bad. I just about suffocated – it felt like drowning except for the heat.'

At about twelve-thirty, when they were both awake but drowsy, the door opened and Perry walked in. 'You guys awake?' he asked breezily.

Charlie swung his legs round and sat up. 'Just about. What's new?'

'Clyne wants a chat with us all in his room. Like now. Yeah, I know it's not three o'clock, but that's what he wants. So put your shirts on – let's go.'

'I sometimes get the feeling you'd do anything for money.'

'Right – and just as well for you, Charlie Thompson.'

Clyne had a large, pleasantly cool room, and they found him seated and relaxed at a bamboo table already chatting with Roz who was sipping a drink. As Perry led the others in, Clyne stood up and moved a step or two towards them. Jonathan was surprised to see he had on a long skirt-like affair in chequered blue and white, worn with a thin, white, open-necked shirt and sandals. 'Come in,' said Clyne amiably. 'Pull up some chairs and let me fix you a drink.'

He poured Mandalay beer for Perry and Charlie and a coke for Jonathan. Clyne smiled at the boy's frank interest in his skirt. 'They call it a "longyi",' he explained. 'Ideal for this climate. You just wind it round you, then tuck it in with a twist in front – you try one when we get to the farm. I'll show you.'

'Thanks,' said Jonathan doubtfully.

'Well, Perry, Charlie, Roz, Jonno,' Clyne said, lifting his glass. 'It's good to see you – your health.' He swallowed a mouthful of whitish fluid. 'Coconut milk,' he explained in a quiet aside. 'Good for the gut.'

Perry raised his own glass and gestured around. 'Here's to you, Walt,' he said, and took a drink. The others drank too (Jonathan feeling silly) and waited in silence.

'I guess I have to start with an apology,' said Clyne after a moment of thought. 'I cut short your rest. Sorry about that – you see I needed the chance to talk kind of privately. Hell, look, I'll put it straight on the line – when I say privately I mean without Joe.'

Jonathan's interest in the situation grew. Something odd was going on, something really peculiar. For a start there was Clyne in his old lady's dress, a very odd ball – look at him. Short grey hair with a bald patch like a monk's, unframed glasses, very tanned, burnt by what must have been years in the sun; softly spoken, dreamy looking sometimes, just not tuned in at all, although that was probably misleading; he probably was tuned in, very much so, a very deep thinker. Hard to put an age on him – anything from forty to fifty-five, maybe more than fifty-five. Clyne. A very odd ball! Clyne and Bergman – oh boy, what a pair. And now a secret coming out of the bag, something Bergman mustn't know about.

He glanced at Charlie – he was playing the hairs of his moustache along the rim of the glass and looking intense, not missing a move. No doubt about Charlie's interest.

'Perry,' said Clyne, 'You know something of my work here, in Burma, you know the essence of it don't you?'

'I'd hardly say that, Walt,' murmured Perry twisting his glass one way then the other. 'It's been a long time. I'm a bit out of touch. I know you got yourself a deal with the Burmese authorities. I know about the farm out east in Shan there. I know you're doing new work. That's about all.'

Clyne turned to the others. 'I don't want to bore you with details,' he said. 'Anyway, Joe may come back any minute, so I've got to be quick. But I lived once in Massachusetts, United States, and I studied – later taught – experimental agriculture. Trying to get more out of a given piece of land, that was my whole aim. Better crops, fatter animals, faster growth – and with it all, conservation. You know the good soil, good growing soil with all the vital nutrients in it, is topsoil. Well, if you leave the job to nature it can take a thousand years for a one-inch layer of topsoil to form. And then, if you don't take care of it, the winds can blow it away in just a year or two. That's called erosion.' He lifted his eyebrows at Jonathan, to Jonathan's considerable displeasure. There was no mistaking the sign. This was like old Harrap in Geography. 'You've heard about erosion, Jonno?' Clyne asked.

'Yes,' said Jonathan grimly. 'A bit.'

'Good, good. Always take care of your topsoil. I call that the first law of agronomics.'

Jonathan's interest went quickly downhill. Silly old spad.

Like the ticking of a clock Clyne's quiet, precisely articulated voice went restlessly on. 'After a while I longed for a chance to put my knowledge to a severe test, to put it to work where it could do great good for mankind. And I confess I wanted a change of lifestyle too, a strangely strong sense that I should go. I think I knew the same awareness of being called that missionaries must feel, the same absolute compulsion, the same belief in destiny and duty – although I hasten to say I'm not of a religious turn of mind, not in the ordinary meaning of the term at least. Be that as it may, I began to think of Burma and its great, mysterious interior. You see, Burma has not had it easy – internal wars between kingdoms, wars with the English, Dutch and Portuguese, occupation during the war of 1939, political unrest, much poverty and so on. Quite suddenly I saw that my future would be here no matter what.'

Jonathan wriggled in his bamboo chair, then scratched the back of his left knee with his right fingers. Given a little bit of luck Bergman might come back, that would put an end to all this. Oh God, the eyebrows were coming his way again. Yes, here they were, all arched and threatening – and now the question.

'Do you know when Burma became independent, Jonno?'

'No. And can I have another coke, please?'

'Oh, ah, surely, surely. Perhaps the rest of you would like . . .'

'No thanks,' said Roz looking levelly at Jonno. 'And Jonathan can pour his own.' There it was, the little warning, the formal 'Jonathan'. He walked quietly to the drinks tray and poured a coke with exceptional care. He'd thrown boring old Clyne for a moment and that was enough.

'Go on, Walt,' said Perry. 'We'd like to hear it all.'

Clyne nodded gratefully, sipped another dram of coconut milk, and continued. 'Burma became an independent nation in 1948. It flew its own flag – red with a blue square in the upper left corner, and a big white star and five small ones. It's a nice flag – you'll see it around the place. Those stars on the blue corner – they're very symbolic. The big one, you see, it stands for the Union of Burma, then the little ones all clustered round it, they're for the main nationalities of the country – Shan, Kachin, Karen, Chin and, of course Burmese. Yes, a nice flag. But I guess all emerging countries have a shock or two coming to them – freedom is a great thing but it sure as hell doesn't promise the streets will flow with milk and honey, *no* sir. When the flag-waving finished, poor Burma found itself facing immense problems – just about insurmountable they must have seemed at the time. See, there really wasn't any union at all, just argument and bloodshed. There were impenetrable forests, mountain barriers, unbelievably primitive peoples in some areas – including headhunting tribes by the way – there was poverty, there was, well, you name a problem and Burma had it.'

The reflective eyes came back towards Jonathan just seating himself with the new, loudly fizzing coke. 'You come from the UK, Jonathan. Everybody there speaks one language – English. Right?'

'Some people speak Welsh,' replied Jonathan. 'And some people have accents so strong you can't understand them properly.'

Clyne smiled briefly, accepting the information as well intended. 'Okay. Now consider this. In Burma there are nearly two hundred and fifty languages and dialects, and about a hundred and twenty separate races of people – and even greater numbers of tribes, and a lot of these tribes, these groups, were at each other's throats. Think about that, then remember on top of all this there was an awful lot of politics going on – extreme right and extreme left and a variety of in-betweens, and these pressures, often pumped up by outside powers as you'd expect, blew up into rebellions; really ugly situations. I tell you it was some mess, in a way the kind of mess that appealed to me, led me on more and more irresistibly to the thought that here was a place I could do something good.' He gave a short, soft laugh. 'Don't get me wrong. I don't want to sound like some kind of angel with a doctorate. It was the practical side of things that turned me on. I wanted an identifiable task, then be left to get on with it. Like a boy building a sandcastle on the beach, I guess.'

'You're being very modest,' said Roz gently.

'No, no, I'm not.' He seemed quite agitated about the need to get this right. 'That really is how it was. Just like that.'

Jonathan noticed a gecko clinging to the wall and studied it. Bluish. Interesting little creatures, slung very low and all done up in a sort of armour plate. The gecko went carefully up the wall and part way across the ceiling where it stuck to the plaster without difficulty. Strange pouchy eyes. But now Clyne was droning on again after another deep pause and a couple of sips at the coconut milk. No sign of Bergman coming back. Worse luck.

'Anyhow,' said Clyne, 'to cut what was a heck of a long and complicated story short, in 1962 the army took control and formed a government under a guy named General Ne Win. Later there were elections and this and that and so forth, and Ne Win became President U Ne Win.' Clyne chuckled. 'That "U" often throws foreigners here,' he said. 'It's just a title of respect – you write it with the letter U but pronounce it Oo, the way I'm doing. Yeah, well, I'd been making my name known to some of Ne Win's officials, kind of hard going in those days. They didn't like foreigners too well – maybe they didn't have much reason to – but I somehow knew they'd let me in, and eventually they did. That was way, way back. I tell you, time runs out faster than you think. It's a lot of years I've been here.'

Perry laughed. 'It shows, Walt. You didn't get that suntan from a three week vacation.'

'Right, but say, I'm taking much too long over this explanation. I'll cram the rest of it into a sentence or two, then we'll fill the detail in later. Officials sent me east to the hill country where peasant farmers had been devastating the countryside. Just due to ignorance, of course. They cut trees, dug up good soil, let it blow away, moved on – one long procession of disaster. I set up an experimental farm near the township of Kengtung, and we've had some really good successes – I'll show you when we get there. But one of our biggest problems was transportation. It took months, and I truly mean months, to get stuff in from Mandalay or Rangoon. Livestock died, gear got damaged or lost, vital supplies – fertilizers, weed and pest killers, almost everything arrived spoiled or ruined – it was hopeless. Boy, that was some slow start. Then I persuaded the government to let me have my own little airline.'

'Ah,' said Perry. 'Bergman. That's where he comes in.'

Clyne looked up, an odd expression on his kipper-brown face, almost a sadness. 'Joe comes in just about everywhere,' he murmured. 'He's a great guy. I do my work with the help of eighteen boys – marvellous kids. Joe brought them in. Joe, the kids and, ah . . .' he looked away for a moment '. . . my wife, that's the whole department.' He gave his small smile, aimed shyly at Perry. 'I guess you didn't know about her, Ma Hla, my wife.'

Perry's lean face transformed as a huge, good-natured grin took over. 'Wife? You're darned right I didn't know. Don't tell me Joe found her for you too,' he said.

'No, no. That's something Joe didn't do.'

'And there's me thinking you weren't the marrying kind. Some family, eh? A wife and eighteen kids, just like that. You've been busting through a fence or two since we last met. Most fantastic thing I ever heard.'

'Lucky for me at my time of life,' agreed Clyne, the smile less shy now and seeming set for some time to come. 'Ma Hla, you know, she really is amazing. Beautiful, capable, patient – I just run out of words. Being mother to eighteen kids isn't easy, take it from me. Yes, I've been lucky. Roz, she'll be mighty glad to see you. There's never any female company, and that's hard. Perhaps you can help her, give her a little bit of a rest, and talk and all that. I know it won't be for long but just a few days would be treasured.'

'It will be a great joy for me,' said Roz. 'I can't wait to meet your family. They all sound wonderful.'

'These boys,' said Perry, the grin faded almost to nothing now, and a wholly different expression, searching and less flip, replacing it. 'What ages are they?'

'All between twelve and fourteen, as far as we can tell.'

'Yeah? *As far as you can tell.* What kind of deal is this, Walt? Who are these kids?'

Clyne began to rotate his glass slowly on the table and looked down, away from Perry's sharp eyes. He carried all the outward signs of embarrassment. 'It's a long story,' he said quietly. 'And it brings me back to Joe. Look, there are things I have to say that I think, Perry ... forgive me ... but I think should be private between the two of us; for the moment, I mean. You see, I have to protect Joe.' He looked awkwardly round at the others. 'I hope you understand. I don't mean any disrespect.'

'Don't worry,' said Ros, starting to stand up. 'Have your private talk. As it happens, I'm still tired so I'm going back to my room.'

Then Charlie banged his thighs loudly with the palms of his big hands. 'For me, it's a look round the town,' he said. 'Come on, Captain – on your feet.'

'Perry ...' Roz, standing now, looked at him firmly. 'Have the chat with Walt. We'll catch up on the important bits later. Go on.' So the three of them left the room, Roz to rest and read and maybe contemplate a bit – Roz liked occasional moments for contemplation – and Charlie and Jonno for a quick tour of the strangeness and wonder of Rangoon and its far east charm.

Roz saw the other two to the hotel exit and smiled at the effect on them of the midday sun. Stepping out into the street was like walking into a furnace. 'Blimey,' said Jonathan, instantly pulling off his tee shirt and throwing it back to Roz. '*Blimey* – it's hot!'

'You'll get sun-burnt,' she warned.

'I'll keep in the shade. 'Bye.' They moved off. 'Where are we going, Charlie?'

Charlie thought for a moment. 'In Rangoon you start with the Shwedagon Pagoda, that's where we're going.'

'A sort of church?'

'You could say that. Very old and very famous – which of course means you've never heard of it.'

'How boring. A crummy old church. But that was funny in there, wasn't it, Charlie? Walt's farm and all the rest of it – I mean it sounds really weird, doesn't it?'

'Yep, weird. Look. Across the street – our new friend, Bergman.'

'So it is. Hell's bells, Perry and Walt better get a move on with their talk. What's the matter with him, though? See how he's sort of staggering? Is he ill?'

Charlie slowed his pace and with side glances watched the thin figure across the street moving erratically the other way. 'Don't stare,' he said, 'and drop the questions.'

3 Bergman is sick

They headed towards a little, open-sided, three-wheeled taxi parked at the roadside. The driver, seeing them approach, smiled an unspoken greeting. Five nearly naked boys standing just to the side of the taxi smiled also – then, as Charlie and Jonathan began to climb in, opened fire with powerful water pistols. Bam, bam, jet after jet of cold water landed on Jonathan's bare chest and back; and on Charlie's shirt and lightweight trousers.

Jonno turned to face the boys and dithered at the sight of the looks on their faces – smiles vaster than ever, eyes crinkled up with pleasure. They laughed and chattered, reloaded from water bowls and carried on with rapid fire. 'Watch it, you lot,' said Jonathan darkly, but more in surprise than anger as water streamed down his body. Charlie's clothing was drenched. He turned back from the taxi, scowling.

'What the . . .?' he began. But the driver was still smiling. He put a hand out and pulled at Charlie's soaked sleeve.

'Thingyan,' he said. 'Thingyan.' Then raised a waterproof sheet. The message was clear enough – get inside and under the sheet. As soon as they were aboard, jets of water slapping now onto the sheet that they pulled over their heads, the taxi moved off. They could hear the driver's gurgles of humour.

'Flip me!' said Jonathan. 'They're right nerks here. What d'you reckon that was all about?'

'Flip me, too. I don't ruddy well know!'

The driver still chuckled quietly. 'Where you want to

go?' he asked, more singing than speaking the words.

'Shwedagon Pagoda,' grouched Charlie. 'And what the hell was the water pistol business about?'

'Our custom, sir,' sang the driver. 'April brings in the new year. It is the time of the water festival. Thingyan, sir. You will be wet again.'

They were. Very wet. At an intersection of roads a cascade of water battered through the protective apron. Jonno began to whoop with laughter and Charlie, moustache streaming again, changed mood and laughed with him. They were awash now from head to feet, and decided to put the useless apron inside. Around the slow-moving taxi were bobbing, colourful longyis, shirts, hats and towels on groups of joyful Burmese people hurling water at each other and anyone; ducking, twisting, giggling and squawking. 'Blimey,' yelled Jonathan, 'it's not like this in Burton.' The driver seemed pleased that at last his clients had understood and he laughed even more openly than before.

At the magnificent pagoda, the oldest and biggest of its kind in the world, the clamour of the water-chucking gave way to an impressive quiet. Charlie took his shirt off, wrung it out and pulled it on again. Then they began to climb the southern steps into the pagoda. By the third step, a commanding monk appeared from somewhere and pointed to their feet, then to his own and to the feet of others. Charlie got the message. 'We've got to take our shoes off, Jonno. It looks like another custom.' They took them off and parked them among an assortment of other abandoned shoes. Jonno, not easily impressed by noble architecture or even noble people, reacted to the aura of this magnificent, gilded shrine towering skywards over Rangoon. They climbed to a great, sun-baked open platform so hot it burned their feet and had them hopping about and hissing loudly; then they took shelter in the cool of a prayer hall.

Jonno was awed by the sight of people there, praying and offering flowers to Buddha, and looking serene and at peace – and by the soft sound of bells ringing, liltingly from somewhere unseen, and by the strong sweet smell of incense. But hunger set in.

They went to the shoe park, then to an open-air food stall of wood planks and an old black umbrella fixed high up on a long stick. The umbrella threw a patch of shadow over the goods for sale – fishpaste, rice noodles, shrimps, vegetables and pieces of meat that could have been chicken, or on the other hand, could have been anything else. Not a cheeseburger in sight. Jonathan studied the collection suspiciously, then saw some enormous eggs and decided on one of them, with noodles. The only drink on offer was the juice of sugar cane, so he had some of that. He ate from a crudely made metal spoon and enjoyed his choice. Charlie had shrimps and some sort of shredded salad which he chomped through with frequent pauses to consider the flavour. The proprietor beamed at him hugely, swaying his head and in no way put out by the look of blank gloom signalled back at him by Charlie's sweating face. 'I expect we'll be ill after this,' Charlie said when they finished. 'I'll pay the geezer then let's find a taxi.'

For a time they had forgotten about Bergman – Bergman and his staggering by the hotel – and the mystery behind him. They had forgotten old Clyne, and the farm and Ma Hla and the eighteen boys, and all the rest of it; the whole pack of tricks. But on the way back, Jonathan brought the subject up again. 'We've only got a little while before Clyne wants us. D'you think Bergman will be there?'

'Could be.'

'What d'you reckon is going to *happen*?'

'We're going to eat.'

'Eat? But I feel full.'

'You surprise me.'

'When we get back to the hotel let's find Perry first. And Roz.'

That proved to be easy. Perry and Roz were relaxing together in the hotel lounge, empty cups in front of them. Roz tossed the tee shirt across. 'Put that on,' she said. 'You look like a barbarian. And you've had too much sun, just as I said.' Jonathan put on the shirt and felt better if hotter.

'Join us, gentlemen,' drawled Perry. 'We've had ourselves a little tea party – very Burmese. You want some genuine Burmese tea?'

Charlie lowered himself into a bamboo chair equipped with comfortable cushions. 'No thanks,' he said. 'We've had some genuine Burmese sugar cane juice. What's new, Perry?'

'Since you guys put me into a position of confidence with Clyne, I can't really tell you – can I?'

'Oh! No?'

Peregrene had a way of never letting life overwhelm him – had a light touch to bad news and a basic toughness that helped him take physical or mental stress in his stride; but he was not because of that a man without feeling – and it was clear he felt something now. 'Look, all I can tell you today is that Joe Bergman is sick, a sick man.'

In the act of sitting down, Jonathan paused and leaned across the table at Perry. 'We know,' he said in a stage-like whisper. 'We saw him staggering about, he could hardly walk – we saw him in the street.' He completed the downward movement and sat, alert, chin in cupped hands, waiting.

'Okay, you've seen it. So keep quiet and act normal, and be pally with Bergman; he deserves it, poor guy. We start airlifting tomorrow, but leave all the talk to me. Do you want to wash before we eat? By the way, this lunch could be a long one. Maybe three hours. They're civilized out here.'

Roz got up. 'Back here in ten minutes,' she said. They went off to tidy up and then they drifted back to the lounge. Clyne arrived soon afterwards and led them to the dining room. Dish after dish was brought to the table by an army of attentive, amiable waiters. For Jonno it was the most extraordinary meal of his life, a seemingly endless adventure of flavours, much of it pepperminty-hot which he increasingly realized he liked. They all ate well and the conversation was free-flowing and relaxed, Clyne on specially good form, witty, urbane and quietly entertaining. Not such a bad old nutter maybe, Jonathan reflected, though on the tricky side; someone to keep an eye on.

The meal finished at a little after five and Clyne offered them a sight-seeing tour to be followed, he suggested, by an early bedtime; they would be booking out of the hotel at four-thirty next morning. 'Don't worry,' he said, 'it's not the little taxi this time. I've got hold of a six-seater estate car – every comfort.'

They drove along the shore of Rangoon's Royal Lake where they stopped to look at a weird collection of stalls selling pots and pans in glittering aluminium and brass, animal skins, dolls and other simple toys, books, medicines – almost everything, Jonathan decided, everything that is except anything he would want to buy. As they wandered slowly past the stalls a short but loud scream

came from the end of the row. Jonathan ran forward to investigate and was aghast to find a boy of about his own age being tattooed on the arm. The boy and the tattooist, a quite old man, sat facing each other on mats. There was something relentless about both their faces, and it was clear that although the boy had screamed he was a voluntary victim. They ignored Jonathan who stood quite openly gaping. The man held the boy's arm tightly and pricked away at him with a two-tip needle pushing colours under the skin. Sometimes it seemed to hurt very much, at others not. Then Charlie and Roz arrived beside

Jonno and tugged him gently back towards a stall where Perry was buying a souvenir calendar.

In the car Jonathan let go with a brief burst of feeling. 'That was horrible, that kid being tattooed. He was *screaming* at times.'

Clyne took an easy attitude. 'It's accepted here,' he explained. 'They believe in it. Different tattoos bring different things – good luck, beautiful wives, safety in battle. All you do is name your choice.'

'Nerks,' said Jonathan.

'Yeah,' Charlie agreed. 'Local custom again, eh?'

Clyne gave that flutter of his right hand he'd used before when forming a thought. 'I've learned to treat local customs with a deal of respect,' he said. 'Part of the indigenous culture, you know.' Jonathan instantly switched his mind off.

Rangoon certainly was a vivid and beautiful and different city. Even in the centre, set among big buildings, there were masses of trees which Clyne obligingly identified as mango, palm, tamarind and heaven knows what else. They drove along the shore of a second lake, Inya, where men were wading among water lilies scooping out tiny fish with hand-nets, then visited a huge covered-in market and, after that, passed by a monastery where people in yellow robes stood quietly at the entrance. 'Monks,' said Clyne, slowing the car.

Jonno studied the group with more than usual interest. 'Some of them are only about ten years old,' he said. 'They can't be monks.'

'Truly they are – novice monks. You find them younger than that – some boys go into the monastery at only six or seven. It's a great honour, you know, for the family.'

'Wouldn't suit me,' said Jonathan.

'Right,' agreed Charlie. 'And it wouldn't suit the monastery, either. Five minutes you'd last mate – if that.'

They went to bed soon after eight still tired from the journey and the big time-shift. At four-thirty next morning, Jonathan yawning and sighing, they loaded their gear into the six-seater and headed out through the darkness to Mingaladon airport. They found Bergman already at the Dove and looking different: brisk, authoritative and fit.

4 Let's fly

Two aircraft handlers were loading the last of dozens of large cardboard boxes into the aircraft. 'Chicks,' explained Clyne. 'We're almost loaded.'

Peregrene walked slowly round the Dove looking at it carefully in the half light of early dawn. He went a full circle, finishing at the port main wheel where Bergman crouched, examining the tyre. 'Problem?' asked Perry.

'No. New tyre.'

'How about the starboard motor? All fixed up?'

'Yep, it's okay. We had a break in the throttle linkage.'

'Really? They're, uh, automatic throttles aren't they?'

To Jonathan, listening, it seemed a bit of a loaded question, but he wasn't sure. Bergman dealt with it briefly. 'Right,' was all he said; one word, and rather sharply delivered at that.

Peregrene wrinkled his brow. 'Not nice when a throttle doesn't work,' he said. 'A life shortener, eh? Mind if I fly in the right hand seat, Joe?'

'Go ahead.'

Bergman turned to Clyne. 'Let's fly, Walt,' he said. 'Those chicks are heating up.' The handlers threw securing nets over the stacked boxes and tied them down. As the men scrambled out, Clyne beckoned to Roz, then the others, to go aboard. Seats had been removed from the rear of the aircraft to form a cargo deck, but there were still eight in place, up forward, four on each side of the cabin with a centre aisle. Despite the door and escape hatches being open and some of the passenger air-vents being piped down to the boxes you could feel the heat from so many thousands of tiny bodies.

While Bergman completed the stowage of bags and packages, Perry came aboard, went forward and squeezed himself into the co-pilot's seat. He glanced back into the cabin at Charlie. 'Bit narrow up here,' he said. 'Might have to put you on a diet, Charlie.'

'No,' said Jonathan quickly. 'I'll fly co-pilot instead.' Charlie peered forward, frowning.

'My God,' he muttered, 'a cockpit for pygmies.'

Then Bergman walked up the aisle glancing about him. 'Fasten belts,' he said. 'Walt, I'll leave everything open until we've got the engines running – you close the hatches when we start to roll. Okay?' He'd put a navy-blue jacket on with four gold stripes on the sleeves and, despite an open-necked shirt and battered trousers, looked pretty good. For a moment Charlie's and Jonathan's eyes met and they both knew they were thinking the same thing. Hard to believe this was the man they'd seen lurching past the hotel just hours ago. Bergman slid adroitly into the captain's seat as Perry leaned across towards him – not much of a lean in the narrow configuration of the cockpit.

'Will you talk your way through the drills, Joe? I'd be interested.'

'Sure. Well, I've done the pre-start checks. We've got controls free, trimmers set neutral, brakes on and locked with a bit better than a hundred and fifty pounds of air pressure – see here?' He tapped a gauge near his left knee. 'And we've got twenty-four volts, generator field switches on, rotating beacon and nav lights on. Good, we start the right engine first, so I'm turning on the primer located on my left clockwise – now prime four strokes with the plunger, okay? Now primer anti-clockwise and four strokes for the left intake. Next, both throttles quarter open, mag switches on – and let's hit the start button.' The triple-blade starboard propeller struggled round for one turn, or a turn and a half, then the engine fired and was smoothly away; Joe set the throttle for twelve hundred rpm and quickly started the other engine. Both Gipsy Queens were going well.

Perry's watchful eyes had taken it all in. Perry was a man, if ever there was one, who positively seemed to have been born to fly. It showed all the time. Once Charlie said, 'What a mess you'd be, Perry, if we didn't have aeroplanes – I mean it's not as if you did anything else well. How's the reading and writing coming along, by the way?'

Peregrene had smiled his slow smile and replied, 'If we hadn't had airplanes I don't think we'd have had me – I guess I'd have had to wait around for the day.' No aircraft was a stranger to Perry. 'Jeeze, but airplanes are alive,' he said sometimes. 'Most of my best friends have been airplanes' – and it was only partly a joke.

Already he felt at home in the Dove and liked it. An old aircraft and, yes, a bit narrow, but a good one. Bergman was good, too – something else Peregrene already understood. One able pilot senses another, and it only takes a moment or two to happen. Bergman talked on through the routines. 'We've got good oil pressure, brakes above three hundred pounds, check VHF sets one and two, the navigation aids – ADF, VOR/ILS, marker beacons and gyro compass. All good.' He called ground control for permission to taxi, then released the brakes. Golf-Alpha Romeo Oscar India began to move. Clyne went aft to close the door and hatches, and Jonathan sat enjoying the never-failing thrill that hit him somewhere very deep and hard, but agreeably, at this moment; a sensory process that began when the engines started and built up through each stage of pre-flight readiness to take-off. Take-off was the climax.

Bergman went quickly through the power checks and four minutes after the big Gipsy Queens came to life Oscar India was accelerating down the smooth tarmac of runway zero-three on full power. At seventy-five knots the stick came smoothly back, the aircraft went into 'rotate' and left the ground. Bergman braked the wheels, then selected gear up and settled to an initial climb of ninety knots. At 100 feet he took the flap in and increased speed to 105. The sound level in the cockpit was high, but you could make yourself heard without intercom. Perry turned to Bergman. 'She's going well,' he said.

'Yuh. It's a beautiful machine to fly. Have a go.'

'You bet.' Perry put his hands and feet forward and took control as Bergman relaxed and crossed his arms.

'Level out at six thousand,' Bergman said. 'Stay on this course, zero-three-zero. By the way, there's no autopilot. We fly the hard way.'

'Darn right, too.' The two men looked at each other and grinned. At 6,000 feet Perry levelled out and brought the throttles and pitch controls back to give instrument readings of plus half boost and 2,100 rpm, both engines. The airspeed indicator crept up to 135 knots and stayed there. Bergman nodded approval.

'Hold everything like that,' he said, then yelled at the passengers. 'Take your seatbelts off if you want to. It looks pretty smooth.'

Jonathan bent forward towards the cockpit. 'Can I stand up there, in the doorway?' he asked. 'You know, so I can watch.'

'Sure. D'you like aeroplanes?'

For a moment Jonathan wondered if he'd heard right.

Did he *like* aeroplanes? The same as Peregrene and Charlie, they were more or less what life was for. As he groped for a suitable answer, Perry spoke. 'Jonno's a great aviation man,' he said. 'And, ah, don't let him hear me admit this, but he's actually already a good flier.'

Jonathan arrived in the doorway now, smiling, the flash of indignation gone. Great that Perry had said that. Slowly Bergman turned to look at him and smiled back, a warm approving smile – the man seemed so changed since yesterday. 'How old are you, Jonno?' he asked.

'Thirteen.'

'That's good going, then yeah, I'll say so, good going. You'd better take my seat for a while.'

Jonathan gulped. 'Really? You mean it?'

'Yes. I'll take a rest in the back.'

'Heck, thanks. I'll just get my cushions.'

When he was comfortably settled, one cushion behind and another beneath him, and rudder pedals adjusted for short legs, Perry pointed to the essential instruments and said, blandly, 'You have control', and took his hands and feet off. So Captain Kane was flying again – and from the left, the commander's seat.

'I have her,' he confirmed and put his whole mind to thc job.

In fact Bergman had not gone back for his rest but stood in the doorway watching. 'That's okay,' he said in a while. 'Good speed, good height, good course.' He tapped an instrument with a thin finger. 'D'you know what that is?'

'Yes. The VOR.'

'Right. I set it up on an away radial from Rangoon. The needle's moving left, so what are you going to do?'

'Change course left to centre the needle.'

'That's it. Steer zero-two-zero – we've got some drift on.'

As Jonno came in with a touch of aileron and rudder, Bergman turned his attention to Perry. 'It's pretty well back to the old bush flying days out here,' he said. 'We don't go in much for navigation aids. There's an occasional VOR or ADF beacon in range but you've got to watch them. Always have a map.'

Perry nodded. 'Dead reckoning, prayers and luck, eh?'

'Save your prayers for the monsoon weather. You might need 'em then.'

'Check. Prayers reserved for monsoons.'

Most of the instrumentation and control gear was familiar to Jonathan, but a cage-like device on the panel by Perry's left knee took his eye. 'What's that for?' he asked, pointing.

'Good question. That's the landing gear safety switch,' explained Bergman. 'If you've got weight on the wheels they can't be retracted. See, just once in a while you'll get a pilot select gear up when he means flaps up, and that can be highly embarrassing. It can't happen on this aircraft unless you lift the cage and pull down a switch behind it. Do that and you by-pass the safety circuit – and if you select gear up now you'll sure as hell get it up whatever the situation. Not otherwise. Clever stuff, eh?'

'Yes,' agreed Jonathan.

'We've got a nice aeroplane here – it takes care of you.' Bergman peered ahead. 'See that circle?' he said, nodding forward and directing the question at Peregrene. 'It's a ruddy great clearing among the trees, must be three miles across. God knows what caused it, but it's useful – see I've got it marked on my map.' He unfolded a battered pilot's map of the area and pointed to the heavy black dot he'd made long before.

'Yeah, I see.' Perry studied the map. 'You've got a lot of other landmarks plotted, Joe. Quite a masterpiece.' The map was a mass of little crosses, dots and hand-written notes.

'Huh – it's okay if you can understand it. Say, I believe you're starting up out here in the charter business.' Jonno looked sharply round at Perry's face which he noticed was showing a touch of embarrassment. Rare for Peregrene.

'Oh, thinking about it, that's all. Just a thought.'

'Business drying up in the west, then?'

'It's, ah, patchy.' Jonno had turned back to the flight instruments now but he could still detect it, the awkwardness. 'Comes and goes. You never really know.'

'Well, there's not much doing out here. I suppose you've got some government contracts, have you?'

'Nothing you could, kind of say definite. Not definite. We're, ah, just looking around.'

'Take it from me, you've got to be careful. There's always some fool official trying to put his finger up your nose here. Anyway, if I can help I'd be glad to. I reckon I know just about every square mile of Burma – well, from Rangoon all the way north and east. Not so strong on the west – it's a bit off our beat.'

'I'd be really grateful for a copy of your home-made map.'

'Be my guest.' Bergman smiled, very relaxed in style. 'Look left and you should see Toungoo in a minute or so,' he went on. 'A little township.' Jonno examined the vast carpet of jungle beyond the Dove's port wingtip.

'I think I can see it now,' he said.

Bergman waited a while, scanning the distance himself. 'You're right,' he said at last. 'That's some vision you've got. Just hold this course and height, and don't rely too much on the VOR from here because we'll be flying out of range. I'm going aft for a while – think I'll sit down and chat up that good looking bird.' He nudged Perry playfully.

At eight twenty-five, after two hours and fifty minutes flying time, Oscar India began letting down to the landing strip at Clyne's experimental farm about eight miles south-east of Kengtung. Bergman was up front again and very much in command, Perry watching with the same intensity as before. The last few minutes of the flight had been bumpy due to air turbulence and the Dove jerked about more than ever with the start of the descent. Jonathan had gone back to the cabin seat but strained forward against the seatbelt to see what he could, which was most of the action; in fact everything Bergman did with his right hand, and that included throttles, pitch, flap and gear controls and the stick. With reduced power the speed fell away and at 120 knots Bergman took the flap lever located below the throttles and moved it half way down to a gate-stop. The speed came back to 100 knots now, and they were coming in on a straight approach, descending at 400 feet a minute and still bouncing viciously. Clyne seemed a bit worried about the chicks and kept looking back towards them. The nets were holding well.

Bergman's hand moved to the gear selector set low left on the throttle console; he pushed a combination button and finger grip forward and three red lights showed on the panel. Jonno knew that was the wheels going down and waited for the slight judder as they locked. He couldn't detect any special judder among all the rest of the juddering going on but in a moment the three reds went out and three greens came on – so the landing gear was okay. Now the throttles came back again, first to minus two boost, and finally minus four and a half.

The descent angle was steep and looking ahead you could see the farm, four simple rectangular white buildings, one a good deal larger than the others, and all set quite close together. They had bright red roofs. People were moving towards the buildings from what looked like a series of huge table tops formed in the earth. Jonathan thought it all looked a bit odd. He switched his attention to the Dove again, still doing its jumping-bean trick.

There was another speed drop, down to ninety knots and still descending at 400 feet a minute, a precision approach despite the turbulence, with no fuss, no corrections and the strip dead ahead. Then up came the nose as Oscar India flared out a few feet above the ground, more speed came off and then a gentle rumbling from the main wheels meant they were down. Three or four seconds and the nosewheel made contact. A faultless landing. Jonathan arched his eyebrows briefly at Charlie in appreciation – and Charlie nodded agreement.

'Nice one, Joe,' said Perry.

'Normal,' countered Clyne, laughing lightly. 'Normal for Joe.'

Bergman looked pleased at the compliments but said nothing. He brought the flaps in, taxied over to a bay near the farm buildings where an Agwagon crop duster aircraft was already parked, and switched everything off. It seemed very quiet – except for the cheepings still going on in the back – and the end of the bumping was pleasant. Clyne nipped from his seat and opened the door and hatches, then made a superficial inspection of the chicks. 'On a noise count I'd say most of them are fine,' he said. 'Let's get them out.' He put a short ladder down and climbed to the ground. The others followed, except for Bergman, who stayed aboard to begin untying the nets.

Jonno stood by the aircraft shielding his eyes from the sun and watching the approach of the people he'd seen from the air. They were boys, barefooted, wearing only colourful shorts – and all smiling. Then, from round the corner of a building came a woman, small, dark and extremely beautiful. Easy to see why Clyne reckoned he'd been lucky to find a wife like that. She looked very cool in a longyi and blouse with an orchid in her silk-like black hair. Ma Hla had a natural grace that only oriental people seem to have – the way she walked, the way she waved a greeting, the way she moved a strand of hair back from her eye, it all had this smoothness, like slow motion that wasn't actually slow.

She came first to Clyne and the two embraced briefly. Then she shook hands with the others and listened intently to their names. Bergman, poised in the doorway, said, 'Hi, Ma,' and grinned. She smiled and nodded. Clyne held a cautionary finger in the air.

'I don't recommend anyone else uses just "Ma",' he said. 'Ma Hla doesn't like it, except from Joe.'

The farm boys had gathered round in a semi-circle, and Jonathan realized they were all staring at him with the smiles gone and no particular expression on their faces, but presumably they were surprised to see him. He exchanged stares with four or five pairs of dark eyes, then Clyne waved a hand towards the semi-circle and said loudly, 'Meet the boys – our family.'

As far as Jonathan was concerned, he'd met them enough already. The others smiled, said 'Hi', nodded and generally showed interest.

Bergman put a box at the top of the little ladder, then stuck his head out through the door, his white hair flapping about in a strengthening breeze. 'Come on, you lot – get these chicks out,' he yelled. To Perry he added, 'They only understood about a quarter of what I say but it seems to be enough.' The boys surged forward and Jonathan escaped round by the tail of the aircraft to keep away. They took the boxes one by one and carried them off to a building; Clyne went, too, clucking instructions.

'You come with Ma Hla,' said Ma Hla to Roz. 'And you others, please.' She beckoned to Perry, Charlie and Jonathan. 'I give you hot tea. Hot tea good after journey.' She had exactly the sort of voice you would expect: soft and cooing. They followed her between the chicken barn and a well-windowed building at right angles to it, which Ma Hla explained was where the farm boys slept, then turned left and walked along a grit path beside what was obviously the house. A veranda stretched the full width of the house at the far end and had three steps leading up to it. They climbed the steps then stopped when Ma Hla raised her hand. 'Take shoes off, please,' she said. 'Use slippers.' She pointed to rows of differently sized slippers in a wooden rack, and took a pair herself. After a long fumble (with Charlie complaining under his breath that the Burmese had under-developed feet) they got the slippers on and moved on into a spacious but simple room. There were palm-leaf mats on the floor, three low tables and a well-filled bookcase, but no chairs. One side of the room was curtained off: Ma Hla pulled part of the curtain back to show a little cubicle of a room – 'for sleep', she explained. Judging by the length of the curtaining, there were quite a lot of cubicles, six at least.

One farm boy had followed them and was on the veranda now peeping into the room. Most of the peeping seemed to be directed at Jonathan who became uncomfortably aware of it. At last Ma Hla saw the boy and called out something in an Asian language which sent him running away. 'He problem boy,' she explained, smiling and shaking her head. 'Good boy, but problem.' Jonathan could believe it.

The tea was served with cakes and bananas. Jonathan studied the food disapprovingly, then took a cake which tasted on the sweet side. Still, it was better than nothing, and in the end he ate three more and two bananas.

After about half an hour Clyne came into the room and had some tea. He announced they were scheduled to make a flight to Mandalay, which he hoped wasn't overdoing things. There was a broken drive shaft to deliver and assorted items to bring back. 'I'd like you to come along, Perry,' he said. 'Get to know the route, airport and so forth.'

'That's fine,' Perry replied. 'How about the others?'

'Anybody else who'd like to come is more than welcome.'

Roz decided to stay at the house, which Ma Hla seemed to be grateful for, smiling and nodding to show it. The others went on the trip.

As Bergman came up the centre aisle he stumbled, grabbed Jonathan's shoulder, steadied himelf, muttered an apology and went on forward to the cockpit, taking the captain's seat. Charlie tugged at his moustache and swapped another glance with Jonathan. Nobody spoke. The take-off was normal and, in the air, Bergman handed control to Perry. He and Bergman discussed routeing points and the Dove's flight characteristics, and there didn't seem to be any tension between them; it was Perry who put the aircraft down at Mandalay – a little airport not much bigger than Lonehead. They dropped off the drive shaft, took on heavy sacks of materials, refuelled and were away again, Perry still doing the work. At five twenty-five the Dove rolled into its parking bay at the farm and Perry cut the motors.

Things had been humming along at the house, and Roz met them at the door looking hot but cheerful. 'We're cooking the most fantastic meal,' she said. 'You can all come and help. Ma Hla is putting on a special welcome party and it's for everyone – the farm kids too. Isn't that really something? And don't forget to put your slippers on.'

Jonathan liked the idea of the meal but had huge doubts about the other kids. He went into his cubicle – sharing again with Charlie – and changed his shorts for jeans and a clean shirt. When he came out Roz grabbed him and put him in charge of boiling and straining rice. Incredible amounts of food, including sliced meats and a weird assortment of vegetables, were already set out in dishes – magnificent silver dishes – and Ma Hla was nipping about the kitchen preparing more, all done with speed and neatness; no wasted movement. At last she started carrying the dishes into the main room and called to Bergman to round up the boys. They came through the door padding along softly in bare feet, identically dressed in chequered longyis and white tee shirts. All the oriental gracefulness was showing again, the way they looked, moved, everything. They obviously knew the routine and headed directly for the kitchen, collected a bowl each, then went back to squat on a mat, smiling and chattering to each other happily. Only one boy kept looking at Jonathan: the problem boy.

The meal had begun when Bergman walked in, and gestured a greeting to everyone.

Roz had been looking at the neat brown faces of the farm kids. 'What a super family, Walt,' she said. 'Absolutely great.' She turned to Ma Hla. 'And what a credit they are to you. I just don't know how you do it, truly.'

Ma Hla showed pleasure. 'Thank you,' she said softly. 'We are proud of boys, of big family. Boys are content, you can see.'

'Yes, they're a happy lot. They look so . . .' – Roz groped for the word – '. . . so civilized, so gentle.'

'Gentle?' Ma Hla considered for a moment. 'Boys are good soldiers. We have robbers in Burma, yes? The dacoits, you have heard? Bad men, carry guns, make attack. Our boys guard farm, can fight with guns, knives, judo. Joe trains them.'

Bergman had squeezed himself in among the farm boys to sit down. 'Ma and I have a deal,' he said. 'I show them how, she puts it into words they understand. You should *see* those kids in action. We could have used them in the US Army – I'm telling you.'

The last remark had a quick effect on Charlie. 'You were in the American army?' he asked. Bergman shook his head sideways, then looked down at the floor.

'Well, not really,' he said. 'Strictly unofficial. Know what I wore in my shoulder tabs? Plastic cufflinks.' He laughed at the recollection, and lifted his head. 'They didn't know what the hell to make of me – called me everything from *loo*tenant to colonel. Anyway, let's forget it.'

After the meal, Ma Hla took a party of boys to the kitchen to wash up and make more tea. It eased the congestion in the main room and some mat shifting and spreading out went on. Perry had been quiet through the meal, just exchanging a word now and then with Clyne, and now the two of them went out to the veranda. Jonathan nudged Charlie. 'I'd like to go out there, too,' he whispered.

'Okay, let's go. Haul me up.'

There were a few basket chairs outside where Clyne could relax at the end of a day's work, sipping his coconut milk and contemplating the quietness of the evenings. He and Perry were each sitting in one, and Charlie lowered himself into another. Jonno sat on the floor beside him, resting back against the wall and mentally slowing down. It was cool, dark and smelt of the open countryside. What with all that and a full stomach, life in Burma had its better moments. Then something moved at Jonathan's right and he looked round to see the problem boy kneeling, outlined by the light coming through the doorway. The boy was so close his nose almost touched Jonno's, and he was smiling, his white teeth visible in the darkness. Clearly this was an overture of friendship, so Jonathan cranked up a smile in return. 'Boy's name Tin Win,' said the boy.

'Oh, ah, I'm Jonathan Kane,' responded Jonathan. 'I mean . . . Jonno.'

'Jon No and Tin Win much friendly. Tin Win is me, speaks much English. Joe Bergman much teacher.'

'Great,' murmured Jonathan, with a degree of difficulty. 'Er, this is Charlie.' Charlie was bending forward towards the boy and chuckling.

'Hi, Tin Win,' he said. 'I like your name.'

'Char Lee and Tin Win much friendly,' the boy went on in a soft, high-pitched and expressionless voice.

'Absolutely right, all very, very friendly.'

As Charlie finished speaking a loud crash came from the sitting room followed by Bergman's raised voice; he was swearing. Tin Win vanished through the doorway and Jonathan scrambled to his feet and went after him. Bergman lay spreadeagled on the floor with part of a broken dish still in his right hand. Helped by three boys he struggled up, lurched through the doorway and fell heavily again, this time down the veranda steps to the ground. Some of the boys stood smiling and tapping their heads. Tin Win came to Jonathan's side. 'Farm boys think Joe Bergman mad,' he said. 'Joe sick.'

'You can say that again,' agreed Jonathan. 'Blimey!'

Charlie and Peregrene helped Bergman onto his feet while Clyne bustled anxiously round. 'Let's get the guy to bed,' said Perry. 'Where's he sleeping?'

'In the boys' hut for the moment,' replied Clyne. 'See if you can get him there.'

Charlie, Perry and Clyne were back about ten minutes later to say that Bergman was safely in bed. Clyne asked Ma Hla to send the boys to their hut and, after a few quick words from her in their own language, they filed quietly out into the darkness. The others sat down on the mats for tea, Clyne looking strained and embarrassed. 'I'm sorry about that, uh, incident,' he said. 'I guess Joe's off colour tonight.'

'Walt!' The call was from Perry, and he sounded serious. 'It's time to quit stalling. Tell Roz and these guys the truth, the whole goddam thing.'

5 Fighting for freedom

Clyne stared into his cup for a second or two, then nodded agreement. 'You're right,' he said. 'Entirely right and it's time they knew, time they knew. But, see, you've got to start by understanding Joe. He always was a loner, did things his way, cared a lot about many things – about people, individual freedom – important things. Joe's a man with a big heart, no-one can deny that. So, I'll tell you about him, but get the perspective right.

'Joe made a living flying for anyone who'd pay him – like you, Perry, only without your kind of success; just a pilot for hire. One time he happened to be on charter business in Berlin when the East German frontier guards shot a young guy trying to get through to the West. Joe got a glimpse of the kid being dragged back and, knowing Joe, you can imagine how he felt – madder than hell. Now he'd been concerned already about the American effort in Namkai where things were going really badly. After that young guy got killed in Berlin, Joe decided to go to Namkai to help out; just like that! He couldn't figure why the South Namkais with all the American help weren't doing better and I think he thought he'd show them how to run a faster war. Remember, he wasn't even American – Joe was born and raised in England. I guess he saw it like one of the old-time crusades; he reckoned that with all our faults we've still got personal liberty – and Joe sure needs a hell of a lot of that – and we don't shoot kids for running away. Everything's black or white with him. Some character, eh?'

It was awkward the way Clyne kept looking for responses from people he was speaking to – instead of hurrying on with the point he was making he'd wait for ages, his face swathed in expectation. This time his wife gave him the prop. 'Joe is big character,' she confirmed.

'Right, Ma Hla. A *big* big character. Anyway, he went out, offered his services to the South Namkai government and they hired him right away. I say "hired" – I'm not sure they ever paid him anything, and it isn't an aspect he'd worry much about. I know they gave him some kind of uniform – you remember how he talked about the plastic cufflinks?'

'Yeah,' murmured Perry. 'I liked that.'

'Well, the north was controlled by what was called the People's Liberation Congress, the PLC. They did really bad things – they infiltrated, terrorized, tortured and they slaughtered at random. Talk about butchery! Joe reckons they were tougher on their own people than us. All this made him madder and madder, and I'm telling you he pushed right into the centre of the action. He's told me things he saw and it was rough, rough, rough.'

Clyne seemed to have a long way to go yet, and Jonathan pulled his knees up, rested his chin on them and clasped his arms round his legs. A good position for a long sit.

'All this broke him up pretty badly,' Clyne droned on. 'Nothing seemed to stop the PLC and one day they came busting through the trees where Joe was, and they were killing everything that moved. This is where Joe did something only he would do. He saw a group of terrified little kids all cowered together behind a wall. Also, he saw a military truck with its motor running. He commandeered the truck, packed the kids inside and drove like hell for the airport. He was flying an old DC3 then, and he transferred the kids to it, started up and took off. The control tower went crazy, they fired every red at him they had, but Joe just turned on the power and kept rolling. So far so good, but in the air he had to decide where to go. To keep it short he came to me, a five hundred mile flight. And how about this for a final touch? He actually flew the aircraft to Bangkok later, and left it for the Americans to collect. He just figured it was their equipment and they must have it back. Yep, some guy.'

Roz had sat staring at Clyne utterly absorbed in the story he told. 'I think that's about the most amazing thing I ever heard,' she said. 'And the farm boys, your family, are those kids?'

'Right. About three years older.'

'Fantastic! How did Joe come to know about you and the farm?'

'Ah. I first met Joe at an agricultural conference in Boston. That was, gee, years back. He was crop dusting at the time and we put on a demonstration together – my theory, his practice. He came out to the farm once, a while later, to deliver the old Agwagon out there. I tried to keep him then but couldn't fix the formalities in time. Next thing he was up to his eyeballs in Namkai.'

Ma Hla went deftly round the room now, pouring more tea from an elegant silver pot.

'Go ahead with the story, Walt,' said Perry. 'You can trust everyone here.'

Clyne pointed his face up at the ceiling, then down towards the floor, then to all of them sitting there, his eyes flitting about at random. 'I told you how Joe was badly broken up. He was *very* bad. Well, he came here, and the poor guy used to wake up in the night screaming and sweating. I used to sit like a nursemaid, talking and talking to quiet him down. Then he ... he took to drinking bouts. Whisky, rice alcohol, anything that would blot out the memories for a while. I tried everything I could think of on him, but he did it more and more often. Mind you, he was always sober when he flew, and we struggled on. One day we were en route for Rangoon together when Joe blacked out. Now, I don't know an airplane's controls from a horse's foot – I was in plenty of trouble.' Clyne gave his tight little repeater laugh. 'Guess I invented a whole stack of new aerobatics in the next five minutes. Then Joe surfaced and put the airplane right way up. I remember he said, "How the hell did that happen?" We were in a spiral dive and overspeeding. I didn't know how to answer. See, he had no recollection of the blackout. None.'

'What an experience,' murmured Roz. 'Terrible.'

Charlie's attitude was tougher. 'So Joe's a drunk,' he said. 'You meet 'em everywhere. Good-bye Joe.'

The bluntness of the comment checked Clyne for a while just as he was opening his mouth to speak, but he soon recovered. 'Joe's sick,' he went on, echoing Tin Win's words. 'I know he is because I got him out to Singapore for a physical and the doctor didn't believe in dicking around. Stop drinking alcohol or be dead in a few months – that's what he said. He really put it on the line for Joe. But you can see how effective it was, meaning it hasn't made the slightest difference, no sir. So I reckon it's up to me to get Joe into a clinic for drying out. And he's grounded as from now. I'll tell him in the morning.'

And in the morning Clyne did. He walked Bergman away towards the terraced planting areas, and you didn't need to be clairvoyant to know what was going on.

When Bergman came back he gave the impression that

most of the life had drained out of him. He sat, silent, on the veranda and stared into the distance, pointedly turned away from the steps and door where people were. Jonathan found it embarrassing and asked Charlie to explore the farm with him, mainly to be out of sight and reach of the broken survivor of Namkai.

They headed towards the stores building by the airstrip and poked about among the assortment of equipment inside it; two low power motorcycles, quite old, were propped against the wall, one in pieces but the other looking as if it might be a runner. Piles of brightly coloured farm implements lay about but didn't excite their interest much and they drifted out to the open air again. Clyne's old Land-Rover was parked nearby so they took a stroll round it. Jonathan pointed to a box-like affair on the front seat. 'Hey,' he said. 'A walkie-talkie. D'you think it works?'

'Switch it on and see.'

Jonathan climbed into the Land-Rover and switched on. A red light glowed and some static crackled from the speaker. 'It's live okay,' he said. 'I think I'll make a test call and see what happens.' He pressed the transmit button on the hand-mike and spoke: 'Jonathan Kane to anybody.' He released the button and waited. To his amazement, Perry answered.

'Anybody from Langhorne. Go ahead.'

'Blimey,' said Jonathan, 'It's Perry – how the heck can that be?'

'There's a set in the house – didn't you see it? Clyne switched it on before he went out with Bergman. I expect they've got quite a few sets scattered about to keep in touch. Anyway, go on, answer the man.'

Jonathan pressed the button. 'Er, hullo Perry. We're down here by the Land-Rover.'

'Okay, but don't be long coming back. We've had a call from Walt and he wants a meeting here with all of us at one. Acknowledge.'

Charlie took the mike. 'Understood,' he said, then switched off.

They ambled back to the house to find Bergman gone; which was a relief, especially for Jonno. When Clyne came in he was looking serious, even depressed. 'Where's Joe?' he asked. Nobody knew. 'We'll have to go look for him soon,' he said. 'I want to keep an eye on him until he gets adjusted. Poor Joe's very down right now. Anyway, I thought we should get together to plan the next few days because there's an awful lot to do. We've got five hundred apple tree saplings to collect at Rangoon and, of course, the drive shaft from Mandalay.' Clyne went on and on about all there was to do, and it was plenty. Jonathan had an uncomfortable feeling he might be planting apple trees before long. Something would have to be done about that – maybe he could get himself appointed Land-Rover driver. He waited for a good moment to speak, and it came when Ma Hla offered them all tea or coconut milk.

'Can I drive the Land-Rover, please?' he asked unceremoniously.

'You mean you can drive too?' queried Clyne in surprise. 'Drive and fly?'

'Driving's easy. Easier than flying.'

'You're some go-er for a kid, aren't you?' Jonathan frowned at that word 'kid'. 'It just so happens there's something you can do right now,' went on Clyne. 'Over in the shed, there, you probably saw some smallish spades and forks, about a dozen of each. Did you?'

'Yes, hanging up.'

'Okay. While we gas on here working the programme

out, you load the spades and forks into the car and take them over to the boys. You'll see them up the hill, and there's a dirt road to follow. Can you do that by yourself?'

'You bet.'

'Off you go, then. There's a radio in the car – switch it on so we can talk to you.'

'I know about it. Okay. 'Bye.' With rising spirits he ran down the steps and away across the open space towards the rugged chunk of aluminium, the Land-Rover. He clambered in, switched on the radio, then turned the ignition key and waggled the accelerator. At first try it didn't take, but after another yur-yur-yur of the starter-motor the engine fired and was running pretty well.

He'd brought his cushions with him and what with those, and the seat fully forward, reaching the pedals was no special problem. Move One was to get as close as possible to the spades and forks to make loading easy. After a general look round, he pushed the big clutch pedal, then moved the main gear lever left and forward for first. While easing the clutch experimentally into engagement he heard another motor start up, and he pushed the pedal down again for a think about that. It couldn't be, and yet it was. Oscar India was starting up. But how? Joe was grounded and the others were all at the house. And there went the second engine – both Gipsy Queens now hammering away. He couldn't actually see the Dove for the stores shed, but what he could see was dust, oceans of it, billowing back from the propellers.

Then Perry came through on the radio. 'Jonno, quick, can you block the airstrip with the Jeep? Stop Bergman taking off – but for God's sake don't get hurt.'

Jonno sat paralysed for a moment, his foot pressed down on the clutch, the engine revving. He wasn't aware of it and there was no-one to see, but he'd gone bright red with shock. Now Charlie's voice came on. 'Jonno, try to trap him before he taxis. And keep the passenger side of the car to the aircraft. And if you think you're in danger forget it, let him go.'

The Land-Rover jerked forward as Jonno's foot came clumsily off the pedal. He was too busy to look for the microphone to reply, and just banged the throttle to the boards. At the corner of the shed he made a vicious left turn and hauled the gear lever into second. The old Land-Rover gave another surge, a brutal, transmission-stretching leap, throwing up its own duststorm of spectacular size. A second or two more, with speed still building up and the car screaming away near blow-up point, the Dove taxied forward into view from the lee of the shed. First failure to Jonathan – he hadn't trapped it. Oscar India crossed majestically in front of the Land-Rover, turned left and blew its dust clouds and stones against the windscreen. The noise of the over-stressed Rover engine and spinning Gipsy Queens and the stones chuttering against the car was like a scene from an operatic nightmare.

Jonathan struggled on in pursuit, dust in the car, in his eyes, mouth and throat. He swung out alongside the Dove and slowed down to its speed, keeping station. The dust problem was much less now but the grit was still disgustingly in his mouth and throat. He couldn't see Bergman in the left hand seat so presumed Bergman couldn't see the Land-Rover either. The question was, what next? Charlie and Perry were yelling through the radio. Telling him to pack it in or something. He was still too busy to reply or even think about them. The Dove had to be stopped, and it would be.

The aircraft and the car rolled at about twenty miles

an hour towards the northern end of the strip. Jonathan could see the starboard flap coming down to take-off setting and heard the engine note flatten, first one engine, then the other, and he knew what that was – Bergman checking his pitch controls. There was something unhurried and impressive about the progress of the aircraft, ponderous in a way but no waste of time either, a nice piece of confident, professional airmanship going on. Of course no-one had ever said Bergman was anything but a first class pilot.

The voice on the radio came across more commandingly, Perry's voice. 'Jonno, you are to abandon the pursuit. I say again, abandon the pursuit. Charlie is running out to the Agwagon. Leave the interception to him. Acknowledge.' The boy did hesitate for a second, easing back on the throttle and tempted to obey the call – except what could Charlie do? Moments from now and the Dove would be climbing fast, and the Agwagon didn't have the speed to get near; in any case, even Charlie could hardly do a kamikaze operation to bring it down. Hesitantly he put his hand towards the microphone then, before he found it, the Dove's port engine roared up into high revs and the aircraft began a turn, right. Forward motion had pretty well stopped as the aircraft swung through half a circle. Jonathan wrenched the steering wheel hard round to bring the Land-Rover into the middle of the strip, slammed on the brakes and leapt from the car.

He ducked under the port wingtip, ran for the side door, and hauled it open. The floor was uncomfortably high – no little ladder to help this time – and he leaned inside the cabin, chest on the deck, bottom and legs hanging out, and yelled towards the cockpit. 'Joe, stop!' His voice sounded very shrill and high and oddly cracked

with effort and emotion. 'Joe, *please* stop, they just want to talk to you. They want to ex . . .' It was as far as he got. The starboard engine came on with tremendous power, the brakes hissed and the Dove lurched left, then the port engine went to full power also, and the door pressed back against Jonno's lower half pinching him against the fuselage. He couldn't see the ground but knew what was happening. Bergman had swung the big aircraft past the car and was rolling now for take-off, engines bellowing away in fine pitch and plus three boost. Jonathan did the only thing left to him – he heaved himself inside the aircraft and the door closed. So that was that. He dragged himself forward up the centre aisle and held on to a passenger seat to his right and another to his left, bracing himself againt the acceleration of the aircraft and peering wretchedly through the nearest porthole. They were belting along now and there, just a glimpse, was the Agwagon's propeller starting a feeble rotation. Useless. Charlie might as well forget the pathetic effort – wherever Bergman was going, Jonno was going, too.

Rotate took place smoothly, and Oscar India left the ground. Jonno made his way forward and stood in the doorway of the cockpit. Bergman brought the gear in, then flap, and settled to the standard settings of plus three, twenty-six hundred revs and 110 knots climb speed. Inside Jonathan, fear was spreading; he stood very still, his face pale and mouth dry. There didn't seem to be anything to say.

In the end Bergman spoke, but without looking round and you'd hardly have known he knew it was Jonno who was there. 'You're a fool,' he said. 'In hell's name what are you doing here, Jonno?'

'They told me to stop you.'

Bergman gave him a brief, pinched smile. 'You? *You* stop *me*? Look, the whole goddamn North Namkai Army couldn't stop me, and you say Clyne thought a kid like you could do it?'

They flew on in silence for a while before Jonathan answered. 'Joe, can we please go back?' He asked the question timidly, his voice a bit quavery and tears threatening an embarrassing appearance. 'If we go back Walt won't make any trouble. He ... he just means to help you. He was saying that. Really.'

'I don't need his ruddy help. Don't need anybody's help.' After another pause he pointed to the co-pilot's seat. 'You want to sit up here?' he suggested – and Jonno clambered hesitantly into place. He saw chunky white clouds in a bright blue sky. 5,500 feet, steering two-nine-zero, roughly west.

'Joe, where are we going?'

'Going? We've gone – just about there.' Bergman's hand moved to the throttles and eased them back. Oscar India began a steady descent. At 900 feet the flaps went down to the stage one setting, and soon after that the gear locked into place for landing. Mostly this was forest territory but dead ahead was a large, flat-looking area, yellow in colour and close to a river that seemed to stretch into the distance for ever. Without doubt the yellow patch was where they would land, the only place they possibly could. At 500 feet Bergman pushed the flap past the gatestop and all the way down, and brought the engines back to idle; Oscar India's sink rate now was impressive, she was really losing height at a pace. With the altimeter on fifty feet the fringe trees flashed underneath and behind them, and the stick was coming back for a gentle flare out, then the wheels touched down and Bergman was dabbing the brakes on and off, and on. The aircraft slowed to taxi speed, then Bergman put power on the starboard engine and Oscar India swung left and taxied back along the landing run. A weird corner of the world this, with dry shaley soil, yellow tufts of coarse grass and under-nourished scrubby shrubs, and all round this big, arid patch trees that enclosed it. Bergman eased the aircraft slightly to the right, bobbing over rough spots in the ground. Then, close now to the limit of the clearing, he pushed the left throttle forward and came in with a bootful of rudder and a jab of the thumb brake on the yoke. Oscar India swung right – throwing up more dust and bits of rubbish – and stopped. Bergman locked the brakes on and cut the motors. He and Jonathan sat in silence listening to the high whine of the gyros gliding down the musical scale as they lost rotation speed. Heat built up quickly in the cockpit and Jonno was conscious of starting to sweat.

'Do we get out here?' he asked in a voice that didn't sound like his.

Bergman nodded. 'Yep. We get out here.'

Bergman had folded his forearms across the steering yoke and lowered his head, his chin and under lip pressed against the back of his right hand. His mind seemed to have floated off a million miles away. Jonathan asked, 'What happens now? What happens to me?'

'You?' Bergman raised his head, then reached out and patted the side of Jonathan's knee in an unexpected gesture of friendliness; and when he spoke it was almost with affection, certainly with feeling. 'I'm sorry for you, Jonno, sorry for you.'

The words held menace and beneath the sweat-shine, Jonno turned pale. 'Why ... why be sorry?' he stammered. 'Please, Joe, please – take me back to the farm.'

Bergman shook his head slowly. 'I can't do that, Jonno,' he said. 'I've got a mission to fly and it has to be now. The last important thing for me to do in this life. I'm so goddam sorry for you.'

When the Dove began to taxi from the parking bay at the farm, Charlie had headed for the Agwagon at a faster run than he'd attempted in years. He got the master switch and fuel on, and the engine going within two or three seconds of bounding into the aircraft, short of breath and bright red in the face. As he brought the Continental's revs up, the Dove whipped past on its take-off run. Blindly he taxied to the middle of the strip, dropped flaps for a short-field take-off, made a sharp turn into wind and slammed the throttle forward.

Then something else – fuel. He checked the supply and swore loudly. Three gallons, hardly that. In anguish, Charlie throttled back, taxied to the bay and switched off. Frowning deeply he walked to the Land-Rover and climbed in. Jonno had left the engine running and there was something upsetting and dreadful about that. He drove furiously to the house.

Perry, Roz and Clyne were in earnest conversation by the veranda steps when Charlie arrived. They all looked shocked and there was a lot of agitated hand waving going on, notably from Clyne who was in a hell of a spot. Perry and Roz were insisting he should report the event at once to the authorities. Clyne was like a man in physical agony.

'You see, the authorities here, they're not easy to deal with,' he was saying. 'There's no knowing where this could lead. The end of the farm, end of my family, jail for Joe – you just don't know the way third world officialdom can work – they're small time guys, I'm not blaming them at all, they've got bigger time guys jumping on their backs, but I know the situation. For God's sake try to understand.'

Charlie had the kind of anger that could whip up like a tidal wave, one minute it wasn't there and the next it could engulf an army. 'Clyne, we don't give a damn about your farm or your flaming friend Bergman,' he said loudly. 'We care about Jonno and getting him back and that's *all* we care about, absolutely nothing else! This isn't a craps game we're playing and don't kid yourself we're going to stand around to see how things shake out because we aren't. Now grab that radio and call the authorities. The Dove was heading west. Get going.'

Perry raised a calming right index finger towards the human eruption. 'Charlie's right, Walt,' he said '– if a bit excited. We really do have to call in official help. I mean, you say you haven't the slightest notion where Joe and Jonno have gone, right? And we have to get the kid back fast – right again? The way I figure it that leaves one hope only – a big officially-backed search. So let's use the radio if we've got the range – or we'll drive, or I'll fly you in the Agwagon. We've got to make contact.'

With Roz you nearly always felt that if she didn't have a smile on show at least it wasn't far away. But not now. She was grave and pale and nodding agreement with Perry. 'Face up to it, Walt,' she said. 'Please.'

Then Ma Hla, who had come up among them quietly, began to speak, bobbing her head as she did so, looking as shy as if she almost ought to apologize for the interruption. 'Excuse, please,' she said. 'I think can tell you where Joe goes. Joe has secret place across Salween river. Joe goes there. Ma Hla almost certain. We go. We find Joe, Jonno.'

Clyne gaped at his wife as if she'd just announced she'd swallowed the silver teapot. '*You* know?' he said incredulously. 'But, Ma Hla, how can *you* know?'

'Joe tells me, once Joe takes me there. Joe has guns, grenades there – hopes someday to start new war with North Namkai. I think that. Ma Hla lead you to place. We take farm boys, go there. Take Land-Rovers. We leave now. Two boys stay here, watch farm, other boys with us, take pistols for safety. We leave now.'

She was entirely calm which you couldn't truthfully say for Clyne whose expression seemed more appropriate to the village idiot than a professor of agricultural economics. 'I really don't understand,' he said. 'You've been ... I mean I just don't understand, just don't ...'

Then Charlie let fly with another bit of feeling. 'You can understand later, Clyne,' he said rudely. 'For now let's get the show on the road. What kind of transport have we got?'

Ma Hla answered. 'Two Land-Rovers on farm,' she said. 'One pulls trailer. Some boys in trailer, rest of us in cars. We go soon, now. Walt, bring boys here. We load, take food, fuel, yes? We go.'

Still looking dazed, Clyne walked to the Land-Rover and drove slowly towards the farm boys at work on the raised terraces. Ma Hla turned her gentle smile on Roz. 'Poor husband of Ma Hla, he is surprised. Joe not always talk to him as to Ma Hla.'

'Well, I can understand that,' said Roz. 'You have warmth, Ma Hla. I think you are a healer.' Ma Hla beamed and bobbed at the compliment.

When Clyne came back he was in a second Land-Rover which had some battle scars on it too, like the other one. It towed a long four-wheeled simple trailer with metal hoops spanning from side to side to support a crude canvas cover at present lying folded on the floor. Then, behind came the other car, a boy at the wheel – the problem boy. And with Tin Win were at least five boys who had scrambled in.

For the next half hour or so everybody swirled round the Land-Rovers and trailer in what seemed like galloping confusion, but wasn't. Blankets, baskets of food, fuel, ammunition, a tent, portable lights were all carefully stowed into the vehicles. The guns the boys carried just tucked into the waistbands of their working shorts; a bit casual it seemed to Perry and Charlie who watched one boy drop his, butt first on the ground. Charlie carried an item or two of gear to the cars or trailer where Perry and Clyne worked together to supervise the stowage.

The problem boy came and stood oddly close beside Charlie who gave him a smile and wished he would go away. He said, 'Char Lee Tin Win speaks,' but then he didn't speak, just seemed to stick, which was embarrassing and Charlie fumbled busily with the trailer.

When everything was loaded, Ma Hla and Clyne detailed everybody off to their places in the transporters. Tin Win threw a stuffed sack of something on the driver's seat of the solo Land-Rover, then sat on it and made a test movement of the pedals. 'Heavens!' said Roz, who hadn't seen him at the wheel before, nudging Charlie. 'Is that boy really going to drive?'

Charlie grinned. 'Yep,' he said. 'Tin Win is driving – afraid you might learn something?'

With the loading done, Ma Hla asked Roz and Charlie to ride in Tin Win's car with two farm boys right at the back carrying their light-weight pistols. She reserved the front passenger seat for herself so she could help Tin Win, which put Roz and Charlie in the rear. 'I think I'll keep my eyes closed,' murmured Roz.

Clyne took the wheel of the other car with its trailer and heavy load of gear, fourteen farm boys (the two left behind were sitting philosophically on an old plough, watching) and Perry for company. The problem boy settled onto his sack. 'Tin Win much driver,' he said. 'Joe Bergman much teacher.'

'Tin Win stop bragging,' replied Charlie, 'or Tin Win bally much bore.'

As Ma Hla opened her door to get in, Tin Win said something in the tonal language of Namkai and she nodded, closed it again, and walked back towards Clyne. Next Tin Win spoke to the two boys in the luggage well who scrambled out and stood some yards away. Tin Win faced behind him and stared with strange intensity at

Roz. 'Boy tell,' he said in his small high voice. "Ma Hla much bad. Ma Hla kill Joe. Tin Win know. Tin Win sure. Tin Win, Char Lee, Jon No help Joe.' He turned away and beckoned to the two boys who came running back.

Charlie looked in bewilderment at Roz. 'What the hell is he on about?' he asked.

'I don't know what that means either,' she said.

When Ma Hla arrived a few moments later she had a rifle slung from her slight shoulder. 'We ride with gun in front, guns behind,' she said, settling into the seat. 'Sometimes danger.' Tin Win started the engine, engaged gear and let in the clutch with a massive jerk. Roz rolled worried eyes at Charlie who didn't seem to have noticed Tin Win's much driving and was writing something in big block letters on the palm of his left hand with a ballpoint.

DO YOU BELIEVE TIN WIN? He showed his hand to Roz who considered for a moment.

DON'T ASK ME BUT THINK TIN WIN GOOD BOY, she wrote under the first message. Charlie dropped some spit on his palm and rubbed thoughtfully at the words. They drove for hours across difficult country.

At about four o'clock Ma Hla suggested they should pause for a rest and cup of tea. 'From here is nice country,' she said. 'Is green. Down to Salween river valley. Big trees, rice farms, all nice. Tigers, snakes and wild buffalo not nice – wild buffalo kill even tiger. We keep guns at ready in Salween valley.'

'Maybe you should give me a gun,' suggested Charlie, clambering from the car. 'I can hit a barn door from oh, say three feet.'

She gave her usual little smile. 'Ma Hla keep gun,' she said. 'Ma Hla and boys keep Charlie safe.'

The other car came alongside and stopped, all the boys merrily leaping from the trailer, covered in dust and entirely unconcerned about it. Perry got out, too, looking relaxed. 'Some road eh?' he murmured.

'Tea now,' said Roz. 'Eternal Burmese tea. Then it's on down to the valley where we've got some nice surprises coming – like king cobras and man-eating buffalo.' She lowered her voice to a whisper. 'Charlie and I need a word with you alone. It's important.'

'Come over here with me,' he whispered back. Then, louder, 'I'll swear that's a rhododendron there – how about that?' They ambled towards the big, luxuriously foliated plant, and she told him what Tin Win had said. Charlie picked up bits of rock chipping and examined them with hammed-up interest while Roz talked.

'What d'you think, Perry,' she ended by asking. 'Should we warn Clyne?'

Perry shook his head. 'No,' he said. 'He'd never believe it, would he? And are we even sure we do? I mean, it doesn't sound a very likely situation, does it? No sense and no evidence – just a few words from that funny little fella, Tin Win. Play it very cool, and watch. Come on, let's get that tea.' They strolled back, Charlie carrying a red piece of rock which he showed to Clyne.

'Not worth a dime,' smiled Clyne – 'we've got rubies in Shan but that sure as hell isn't one of them.'

The tea went down well and with it more of the sweet tasting cakes. Ma Hla was briskly and calmly efficient, controlling the boys with ease. Charlie and Roz watched her intently. Could Tin Win have lied about the person who was next best thing to his own mother? Or could he simply be mistaken – could something have been said by someone, perhaps even by Bergman, that could have led the lad to a wrong and terrible conclusion? How much of the problem was the problem boy himself?

Soon after five the cavalcade prepared to roll again, the descent to the greenness and dangers of the Salween ahead. Charlie offered to drive which Tin Win dealt with by climbing into the driver's seat and gripping the wheel defiantly until, at a word from Ma Hla, he started up and jerked the car forward. Clyne had difficulty with his heavy trailer at times, dragging it through rougher and rougher ground and often they had to stop to hack away

at young trees and bamboo and other types of growth, and to drag fallen branches aside. Roz began to feel very weary as they clawed their way forward and she leaned her head against Charlie's ample shoulder. He put an arm round her to help her snuggle against him, and they bumped on. 'My God, I hope Jonno's all right,' he said once.

'So do I. Try not to worry, it doesn't help. Poor little Jonno.'

'If Bergman lets that kid get hurt I'll kill the swine.'

'Ssh. Calm down.'

The river itself was a fine sight; broad, muddy, quite fast moving with islands of rock jutting out at random, and masses of green growth reaching right to the water's edge so densely that the cars had to be parked well back. To the west and east of the river great trees grew from the steep sides of the valley and, looking back, it was hard to see how they'd managed to force their way through at all.

Perry walked over to Roz. 'How are you doing, my little dream girl?' he asked. 'This big lump taking care of you?' He nodded to Charlie.

'I feel, well, just churned up,' replied Roz. 'And tired, oh God, so tired.'

'Never mind, we're going for a cruise – see?' Perry pointed to two rubber boats the boys were inflating with Clyne's help. 'And then, by the look of it, we've got a long walk through the jungle. Great, isn't it?'

6 The jungle prison

'Since you're here, you might as well be useful,' said Bergman to Jonathan. He pointed towards two strange assemblies of metal rods lying along the tops of the left hand row of seats in the passenger cabin. 'Help me get those out – go ahead and open the door. It's too ruddy hot in here anyway.'

Jonno moved along the aisle towards the main door, gazing at the rods as he went. 'What are they?' he asked, sounding suspicious.

'Open the goddam door,' Bergman retorted.

The devices were awkwardly long, ten feet or more, lighter than they looked but by no means easy to man-handle through the doorway, and Jonno had the harder end of it, going backwards. They struggled out with one, then the other, and manoeuvred about until a set of rods was under each wing of the Dove, resting on the ground. 'D'you get it now?' asked Bergman.

Jonathan didn't. 'No,' he said quietly.

'Who's stupid then? They're bomb racks, that's what. Took a heck of a lot of making. Each rack holds two bombs supported on these brackets, see?' He pointed to a pair of trough-like pieces of aluminium. 'Now, this wire cable, here, runs along the front of the rack, and it's fixed to two pins. I take the end of the wire through the fuselage and into the cockpit – got it? And the same for the other rack. All I have to do is pull the wires, one at a time or both together, just depending, and the pins jerk out; when they jerk out the front brackets fall away, and when *they* fall away the bombs drop. Wheeoo-crump! Not bad eh? I've already got lugs fixed to the wings to hold the racks – had that done in Rangoon and old Walt didn't notice – which is just as well. Give me thirty minutes and I'll have this old Dove all kitted out as a low level bomber. The last important thing,' he said, apparently muttering to himself. 'The last important thing to do.'

Jonathan had turned ash white. The man was mad – that was obvious. And he had some utterly mad plan in mind, and he was the kind of madman who would put his madness into action. Jonno knew enough about him to know that. You were supposed to humour mad people – whatever that might mean. Humour them, then try to turn them off some way, and presumably the main thing was to keep chatting, keep friendly. 'I don't see any bombs,' said Jonathan, finding the words extremely difficult to say from nervous tension that dried his mouth and did something uncontrollable to the vocal chords.

'No? Come with me, lad.' Bergman grasped Jonno by the shoulder and held on to him, guiding him towards the fringe trees. 'Keep your eyes wide open for snakes,' he added. 'Miss one and you're dead.' They walked a few yards along a track, Jonno leading but being steered by the strong hand. A log cabin had been built among the trees and cleverly covered by interlocked branches and creepers trained to grow over the structure. Bergman opened a door and they stepped through. 'This is the armoury, Jonno, and there are your bombs.' Eight of them lay side by side on a massive table; they were painted green but had shiny, steel-like noses. 'Two hundred pounders, babies by modern standards, but they'll do what I want them to do.' They looked enormous to Jonno and sinister beyond description.

'Pity about the rest of it,' Bergman went chattily on. 'Those racks over there have repeater carbines in them, twenty-five guns, all ex US Marines equipment, and all ready for action; then I've got a couple of hundred grenades, and a dozen mortars complete with shells and, oh, a hell of a lot of other stuff. Enough for an army, a really good, hand-picked army of eighteen, young, fit determined men. And now time has run out on me. The men are still boys, just boys, full of heart but too young, too young. So it's been a lot of wasted effort. But it leaves the bombs, and the Dove, and one last chance. Now, let's get back, get those racks fixed.' Jonathan felt the hand on his quivering shoulder again, and then they were out among the trees.

Some of the worst of the mind-fogging panic left him as he stood by the Dove watching Bergman take a bottle of whisky and some spanners from a brown hold-all, which he dumped on the ground. He realized he'd said nothing in five or six minutes to humour the madman – say something, stay friends, keep in contact. 'Joe,' he said in the same strained voice. 'Who are you going to bomb?'

Bergman sank some whisky, neat, and put the bottle down. 'If you haven't guessed that then you're not as bright as I thought – but then I don't know how much you've been told. Jonno, I'm going to bomb the thug-leaders of the North Namkai Army – members of the so-called People's Liberation Congress, and maybe the nastiest human beings to disfigure the world we live in, since Genghis Khan and his mob of heavies. Liberation? I'll tell you what the PLC's version of liberty is; it's don't waste the ammo – bury these men alive; it's get out of your houses and live in the fields; it's a rifle butt to the chin; it's get down on your knees I'm the new boss. Yeah, and it's keep the world out so nobody sees. They think it's over. Well, it isn't quite, see? Joe Bergman has a last little bill to present. I'm going back to Namkai, to its capital Han Phnom, to a particular building there and I'm going to drop my regards, all four of 'em, and maybe eight if I get a second run. A last account for what they did to their own people – and to others who just happened to be neighbours. And I've taken steps to make sure the world knows all about it – that's the best bit. Just about everything I saw the PLC do I've written down, some sweat that was, and it's safe with Ma Hla. When I've finished my mission over Han Phnom it'll make headlines everywhere – remind the world of things it should never forget.' He took another longish swig at the neat whisky, then put the bottle back in the bag. 'Come on, let's get those racks fixed,' he said.

Bergman had it all worked out – hand pulled trolleys to carry the bombs, jacks to lift them into position. Jonathan helped to some extent because it was awkward not to. Bergman even topped the fuel tanks up from a string of jerrycans; the man seemed quite tireless, the sweat pouring off him. He was buoyantly cheerful, too, even whistling at times when he had the breath.

During the later stages of getting things ready, Jonno sat on an empty jerrycan and watched. He studied the great, encircling jungle that made an open prison of the clearing, and the Dove – looking dreadful with its bombs in place – and felt deeply afraid. Eventually, Bergman came over to squat beside him. 'Well, Jonno,' he said.

'Well what?'

'Time to choose. I'll give you a compass and you just keep heading east until you find people, or you come with me on the mission. But either way I think you'll die, so if you believe in God or anything...' He ran out of words for a moment then added, 'I'm truly sorry.'

Anger flashed through Jonathan. 'If you're so sorry you don't have to do it! If you're so sorry you can just take me back to the farm, can't you?'

Bergman shook his head, and he did look grave and sorry. 'This is bigger than a couple of lives, Jonno, even if the lives are ours. I realize you won't understand, and we're out of talking time; it's a long flight. Decide.'

'You're mad. You need proper sights and everything – you'll never hit the target.'

'I will – fair and square. I'm going in low, rooftop stuff.'

'They'll shoot us down.'

'Maybe. Decide!' The word swelled and hurt like something physical in Jonathan's mind. Decide. Decide. After another brief look at the unfathomable jungle, he did, his voice fading to a whisper.

'I'll go with you.'

'Okay.' Bergman took a piece of cord from his trouser pocket. 'Hold your hands out.' Jonathan looked blank. 'Hold them out,' Bergman repeated, 'palms facing.' The small, trembling hands came forward and Bergman tied the wrists together firmly but not to the point of causing pain. 'I have to do that, Jonno,' he said. 'I promise I'll untie you when we reach the target area. Get into the aircraft, sit in the co-pilot's seat.' They walked to Oscar India and Bergman helped the boy up the step, followed him in and secured the door. Together they went forward to the cockpit and clambered into the pilots' seats. Jonathan sat with his hands wedged between his knees, shoulders slumped and head low.

The attitude of Bergman was different and remarkable. He seemed suddenly stripped of all cares and uncertainties, deeply relaxed and confident; a man, perhaps, who foresaw death and found it unfrightening and, with that fear gone, had only a sense of purpose left. The Gipsy Queens bellowed into action and Oscar India had come to life again, quivering with power and eagerness. He warmed the engines, ran through the pre-flight checks, then released the brakes and the Dove began to rock gently over the rough ground towards the start of the take-off run.

'I haven't got my seatbelt on,' Jonathan complained.

'Put it on then.'

'I can't with my hands tied.'

Bergman closed the throttles, leaned across, tugged the belt across the boy's lap and locked it; then Oscar India began to taxi again, a jerky motion like a small ship in choppy waters. Jonno was without the cushions he always used when flying so he couldn't see much outside except upwards, towards the blue sky and distant green trees of his prison. He was wretchedly aware of the two bombs beside him. The releasing wire passed under his legs to within reach of Bergman, and he looked at it, hating and fearing it. Next he looked at the panel – all engine instruments nicely in the green – and the flight controls, the pitch, flap lever, everything set for go. Bergman adroitly refolded a pilot's map and put it on the floor between them. 'Okay,' he said, 'let's roll,' and began to ease the throttles forward.

The finality of the moment, the brief words, the power going on, the map, the hateful wire, everything brought a new surge of horror through Jonathan, a surge that joined with the surge of sound from the Gipsy Queens as the throttles reached the stops. He sat rigid for a while until one word screamed out of him – *'No.'* Jonno jerked his tied hands towards the gear selector, then remembered through a vividness of terror that that wouldn't work with the weight on the wheels, then remembered the cage and the safety-circuit breaker switch behind it just above his left knee, and made a dart for it. He lifted the cage, banged the switch down and before Bergman understood what was happening, pressed the lock button on the gear selector and pulled back. They were moving at almost forty knots when the gear collapsed and Oscar India settled down on her belly like a bird with broken legs.

Only then, as the belly of the aircraft was striking the ground, did it occur to Jonathan to wonder if the bombs would explode. That fright, at least, was short lived; they didn't. Instead the roaring engines fell suddenly quiet as the propellers stopped and buckled on impact, and the heavy aircraft slid on to plough a leisurely furrow across the wide savannah. Right at the end of the slide she put her left wing-tip quite gently on the ground and stopped. The bombing mission was over.

Jonathan, sweat-covered, pale and still trembling looked across at Bergman. What now? What would the madman do – beat him, kill him maybe from the fury of this final frustration? Bergman's first move, done automatically it seemed, was to reach to the co-pilot's side of the cockpit and flip a switch, the master switch. Jonathan understood the reason: it cut the whole of the electrical system dead and reduced the risk of fire. Then Bergman crossed his arms over the steering yoke the way he'd done before, lowered his head to rest it on them, and sat motionless.

Bergman sat like a figure of wax.

'Will you untie me?'

But still nothing; no word, no movement. Jonno moved his hands over and touched Bergman's forehead with his fingertips. At this physical contact, Bergman sat slowly up, looked at the hands, then untied them.

'Thanks, Joe, thanks.' What a moment! Not just the relief of having your hands free but the forgiveness that must lie behind it. So maybe he wasn't going to be killed, or thumped, or, anything like that. A new thought came: Jonathan unclasped his lap belt, went through to the cabin and brought back the bottle of whisky. 'Have a drink, Joe,' he said. Bergman took the bottle, then clambered out of the cockpit and went aft to be more comfortable in a passenger's seat. He took a long drink, and then another. Jonathan went all the way to the rear – oddly difficult with the tilt of the aircraft – and opened the main door to let the fresh air in.

Looking back he saw Bergman raise the bottle a third time. Without much thought to it, acting from some inner control, Jonno walked back to the man and took hold of the bottle at the moment of swallowing. Gently he pulled it away, and Bergman didn't resist. 'Have some more later,' said the boy, sounding like a nurse addressing a child patient. 'That's enough for now.' He found the top, screwed it on and stowed the bottle away out of sight in the holdall. Bergman still said nothing but watched the movements vaguely; after the bottle disappeared he closed his eyes and seemed to fall asleep. Jonno studied him uncertainly for a while, then decided to have a look at the outside of Oscar India, at the damage he'd done. The outer bomb from the left hand wing had come away and was lying thirty or forty yards back from the aircraft, and there were bits of metal and fabric spread along the great scar in the ground the old Dove had scraped.

He walked round by the wingtip and examined the damage there, then on to the nose, pausing for a look at the grotesquely twisted propellers. The starboard wing was okay, raking upwards as if Oscar India were banking for a turn, the threatening bombs in place. He wandered along the starboard side of the fuselage, stood by the tail which had a buckled left elevator and damage again to the tip. Then he was back at the door, the tour completed.

Jonno put his head inside and looked forward. Bergman was still asleep or seemed so. One new problem had already come up: thirst. Jonathan had to have some water, but was there any? He tested a cupboard-like door at the rear of the cabin and found it locked. Next, he went cautiously up to Bergman and looked at him closely. The man's eyes were shut and his mouth half open; by no means looking his best. 'Joe,' whispered Jonathan urgently. No answer. 'Joe,' a bit louder this time. The eyes remained shut.

He rummaged in the holdall which had several bottles of whisky in it and a curious cloth-covered metal container with a cork in the top. The cork came out with a plopping noise and he sniffed at the spout, fearing to smell whisky again, or rice alcohol – anything but what he wanted. There was no smell. He tilted the bottle to his lips and out came the priceless luxury of water, fresh and sweet. He swallowed with delight. Better not take too much though – who could say how long this had to last? He put the cork back and went aft again, glancing uneasily at Bergman as he passed him.

God knows what next. He stretched out on the carpeted floor, lying on his back near the door where air currents riffled in and out pleasantly. What he had to do now was to think. Think and think his way out of the mess. On the good side they had guns, a compass, less than, say a hundred miles to go to reach the farm; working together they could surely do it, track their way back, shoot their way out of danger. But on the bad side there was Bergman; unpredictable, drunk, probably mad.

Jonathan yawned, closed his eyes to go on with the big think. When he opened them again, daylight was fading. He had the certain feeling that a gunshot had woken him and sat up in a state of confusion and shock. It all came cruelly back. The crash, Bergman, the bombs. He must have been asleep for ages. Bergman – he looked towards the cabin front and the man wasn't there. God, had Bergman shot himself? A new fear came back and a desperate loneliness. He scrambled out through the door and the loneliness promptly went. Bergman was there, sitting on the grass leaning against the side of Oscar India; he had the holdall beside him, a whisky bottle in his hand, his eyes shut again. Jonathan stood staring down at him. 'Joe!' he said.

'That's me.' The eyes opened redly.

'Are you ... are you drunk?'

Bergman turned to look at the boy, a loose smile on his face. 'I guess I'm a teeny bit over the hill, Jonno,' he said. 'Best way to be you know. Have some.' He held the whisky bottle out.

'No thanks.'

'That's perfec'ly all right. Nobody has to do what he doesn't want to do.' He gulped some more from the bottle, then put it down at arm's length.

'Joe – let's plan how we get out of here and back to the farm. We've got guns in your shed there, haven't we? And the compass you said I could have. Let's make a start, Joe, let's head for the farm.'

'I just said nobody has to do what he doesn't wanna do, and I don't wanna do that.'

'But . . . but we can't just sit here for ever. We can't just sit here until we die.'

Bergman gave him the loose smile again. 'Yes we can,' he said.

'Joe, please!' Jonathan took a pace towards the man and knelt before him, between Bergman's splayed out legs. 'Please help me get out of here. Please.'

'You've spoiled everything,' Bergman muttered. 'Everything.'

'I'm sorry about the Dove. I . . . I had to do something. I was desperate, we'd have been killed, honestly Joe, it was crazy, they'd have shot us down, so it wouldn't have done any good. But I'm really sorry about the Dove, really. Oh God, what a mess it all is!'

Bergman stared at the trembling boy for a while. 'I don't care about the Dove,' he said. 'Not much. It isn't that. Hell, I've screwed up everything else I ever tried, so tell me why the bombing run should work out. Not a chance, Jonno, not a ruddy chance. Know what? The lousy bombs would've fallen off before we'd got there, something would've happened, something crazy, believe me. No, it isn't that.'

To Jonathan's fear now came bewilderment. 'Well what then? What else have I spoiled?'

‘Ah.’ Bergman reached for the bottle again, and Jonathan gently tried to stop it arriving.

‘Please don’t drink any more,’ he pleaded.

‘Shut up,’ said Bergman pulling the bottle to his mouth and taking another swallow. ‘Here, have some,’ he went on a moment later, ‘might do you some good, you’re looking real jumpy, cure those sh’shakes.’ Jonathan lowered his head and kept silent. ‘No, fact is I’d be happy to die here. That’s what you’ve spoiled. See this?’

He held up a capsule, like an antibiotic pill. ‘I had this in Namkai. One little crunch and you’re dead. Used to be cyanide, this is better, doesn’t hurt – that’s what they say. Hell, I’m going to hiccup.’ He hiccupped. ‘So I thought I’ll just sit here and have a little drink and when I’m ready I’ll take my pill – and ex ... exit Joe Bergman. Then I thought, I thought, there’s that kid. So then I thought I can shoot him, save him from being eaten, starving – bad waysh to go, bad bad ways those. But I couldn’t shoot you when I saw you asleep, shee? Another failure, and your fault. So you’ve spoiled it all. Can’t even crunch my little pill.’

Vaguely Jonathan comprehended there was something in a way to be grateful for here. Bergman had deferred his chosen appointment with death so as not to leave a boy alone, a boy who’d spoiled everything. How do you follow chivalry like that flowering so unexpectedly from derangement and despair? He swivelled round off his knees to sit beside the man, the fear easing.

‘I’m glad you haven’t crunched the pill, Joe. There isn’t any need for that. And you’re *not* a failure – think of all the things you did in Namkai, really brave things. And all the farmboys, you’re sort of their father because you saved them, and think how they’ll miss you. So will Ma Hla and Walt. I’ll bet you’ve got friends everywhere who'll miss you. Can I, er, have a drink of your whisky?'

'Uh?'

'I'm getting cold. My legs are cold.'

'Kid your age shouldn't drink whisky.'

'Just a little bit, to warm me up.' Still looking woodenly surprised, Bergman handed the bottle over. 'Watch this, Joe,' Jonathan said, then stood up and hurled the bottle as far as he could towards the distant trees.

'Wha-the-hell-you-do-that-for?' asked Bergman in more surprise.

'You know very well why, Joe,' Jonathan said. 'Now, you pull yourself together. I know you can do it. We'd better spend the night here I suppose – a bit late to start off on foot. We'll leave at dawn. Is there anything we can eat? A meal would really do us good and, blimey, am I hungry!' He was beginning to feel better, the long fright continuing to diminish.

'There isn't any food here.' Bergman gurgled with laughter. 'Losh of fish in the river if you wanna go fishing.'

Jonathan's rising hopes checked for a moment. 'We'll just have to go hungry tonight, then,' he said stoically. 'Maybe we *could* catch a fish in the morning. Let's settle down for tonight in the cabin.'

'Don't go in there.'

'Why not?'

'A snake just went in. They like warm places.' Bergman took another bottle from the holdall and stood up, leaning back against the aircraft for support. He broke the seal, unscrewed the top and swigged away. Jonathan was deeply dismayed at the sudden reverse.

'A snake?' he asked incredulously. 'You're having me on.'

'A sh . . . nake,' confirmed Bergman and gurgled again.

'You go in there and you'll be shleeping with a shnake. Friendly fellas these shnakes, coil round you and hoo hoo hoo.'

'I don't believe you. You're seeing things.'

'Go inshide then. 'S-all right with me. I can just crunch my lovely lill pill.'

Jonathan sat wearily down on the ground again, all the old fear and depression rushing back. A moment later and Bergman stumbled into him, first knocking him sideways, then falling, his full weight on top of the stunned boy. For a a second or two they lay there, motionless. Then Jonathan screamed, and through the screams, shouted at Bergman to get off him, and while screaming and shouting fought to get free. He crawled away breathless and sobbing to sit alone near the nose of the aircraft. Slowly he recovered partial control of himself. This was terrible, the horror of nightmares – and real. He looked back at Bergman who seemed to be out cold. After a while, trembling from shock and chill, he crept towards the holdall and snatched out three new bottles, unscrewed the tops and poured the strong smelling liquor onto the ground. Bergman might still crunch his pill but the drinking – that at least – was over. He hid the bag round at the blind side of the aircraft and decided to stay there, out of sight of his drunken companion. It had become dark. He sat, staring into the night, knees up to his chin, arms wrapped round his bare legs in an attempt to keep warm. Sleep, of course, was out of the question.

After what seemed eternity he saw pinpoints of light in the darkness, then heard a grunt. New terror took charge of him – there was an animal on the prowl and it wasn't far away. He fled round the nose and back to Bergman who had shifted his position and was looking almost comfortable, lying on his side. Jonno sat close to him from companionship and let misery capture his heart. Later he lay down beside the man for warmth, and tried to sleep.

Until dawn there was nothing to be done. And then? God, what a mess.

7 A wrong way to help

Clyne, standing by the water's edge, explained how they would cross the Salween. The heavy duty rubber dinghy was a sizeable affair, about ten feet long and with enough room for three adults in comfort, or three adults plus three or four kids at a knee-banging squeeze. If anything went wrong, there was the second and smaller boat in reserve.

'We have a kind of peculiar way with rivers like this,' Clyne said, a touch of the classroom showing again. 'The current flows too fast to row or paddle the whole way across, so we use a couple of folding anchors. We throw an anchor, test it's got a good grip, then pull ourselves towards it, right? Then we throw a second anchor, haul ourselves over the first which pulls free quite easily from directly above. We repeat the process until we've gone the distance. Of course we have paddles, too, and a pole; also a reserve anchor because just now and again we have to cut one free. Now, ah, you'll see we have a line tied to the back of the boat. I'd like you to hold it and pay it out as we advance. If things really go wrong, I'll holler and you winch us back in as fast as you can. Is that clear?'

'Yeah, it's clear,' said Perry, 'and it sounds rough. Who's making the trip?'

'Tin Win and me – that boy there.' He pointed to a small brown and smiling face.

'Uhuh, we know Tin Win. But, look, let me stand in for him. Walt, it's you and me.'

Clyne had strong moments, and this was one of them.

'Thanks, Perry, but no. Tin Win and I've done this before; we take the boat. And when we're safely across I want the line you're holding secured to a tree. We'll do the same on the other bank. Then we take a loop from the front of the boat over the line and the same thing at the stern – and we've gotten ourselves a kind of floating bridge. We just paddle to and fro along the line – okay?'

A minute or two later the boat was making its erratic first journey across the big river. Clyne had a better throw than you'd have expected – fifty feet a time or thereabouts. The four-pointed anchor with its thin, white nylon line would fly ahead and splash into the water, then the two heads would start bobbing about with the effort of pulling, and the heavier line would slide out through Perry and Charlie's hands. There seemed to be difficulty for a few moments in about mid-river when they were a long time freeing an anchor, then on went the line running slowly out.

'Walt must be tired,' murmured Roz sympathetically at the finish of the trip.

'Darn sure I would be,' agreed Charlie. 'They've been, what, forty, forty-five minutes? He's a wiry old beggar, that.'

Wiry perhaps, but Clyne evidently was tired by the time he got ashore. They saw him fix the main line on the far bank, then lie down to rest. Tin Win came merrily paddling back, the boat virtually hanging from the long line stretched across the river and curving downstream from the tug of the current. Perry and Charlie began to tie their end to a convenient tree, Charlie doing most of the looping and threading of the line, and not doing it very neatly.

Including Clyne's first crossing, the boat had to make four double journeys and a single one to get everybody to the other bank. Roz went with Perry and four farmboys on the third trip, feeling and showing unease as the water flapped the side of the frail craft. The boy rowing – not Tin Win who was on the other bank with Clyne – didn't really have room or strength enough to work the paddles efficiently. One of the other boys, trying to help, snatched the rope to pull them along, but almost pulled himself out of the boat instead. Perry grabbed the boy's legs and hauled him inboard again, the boat tipping dangerously from all the throwing about of bodyweight. Roz closed her eyes until the drama was over. 'Good grief, Perry,' she murmured.

The boys were all laughing, including the one who'd almost gone over. His gun had fallen into the well of the boat, and Perry picked it up. 'Haven't come across one of these in a long while,' he said, turning the gun over in his hands while its smiling owner watched. 'That's an old Japanese Nambu eight millimetre.' He winced, though, when he handed the gun back and saw the boy tuck it in between his waistband and bare brown stomach.

'If one of those guns goes off . . .' The sentence ended in a headshake.

Charlie, Ma Hla and the last two boys came over in comparative comfort on the final trip. They had five machetes with them for hacking at undergrowth, and Ma Hla had her rifle slung from her shoulder. All the boys helped pull the boat out of the water, swarming about like excited ants and falling over each other's feet; they dumped the boat some way up the bank for safety. Clyne and Ma Hla led the advance, each slicing away with a machete. This side of the river was even more densely overgrown than the other, so progress was slow.

In a while the going became easier, the trees more widely spaced and the undergrowth thinning out. Perry, suddenly serious, took a firm grip of Roz's hand and waited until Charlie caught up. 'I reckon it'll be dark soon, Charlie,' he said. 'What about that?' Charlie scowled at the forest, breathing hard.

'These godawful trees,' he said. 'You're probably right. What the hell are we going to do?'

Then they realised that Ma Hla and Clyne had stopped the advance, and something was going on up at the front. They pushed forward to see a boy climbing a tall tree. He did it with impressive agility, scrambling upward from branch to branch at speed, finishing near the top with his arms clinging round the narrowed and swaying trunk. In a moment he started down – the same sure-footed confidence. On the ground he spoke rapidly to Ma Hla who, for once, showed feeling, a sort of weary sadness. 'Ma Hla sorry,' she said, speaking mainly towards Roz, but glancing at Perry, Charlie and Clyne, too. 'We come wrong way. Very sorry, and dark soon. We go back and think plans. Ma Hla very sorry.' Then she spoke to the boys, more loudly and in their own tongue. Gloomily Clyne and a number of boys began wandering back the way they had come. Ma Hla and the others followed.

At that moment Charlie saw Tin Win standing there, just looking at him; and there was something powerful and peculiar about the look. Charlie stared back into the bright eyes. The problem boy spoke. 'Tin Win climb tree.' Perry and Roz were starting to walk very slowly towards the river, and they stopped now and turned to listen. Tin Win gestured them away. 'You go, you go,' he hissed. 'And Char Lee go. Tin Win stay, climb tree.'

A glow of feeling was coming over Charlie and it showed. 'Tin Win much friend,' he said. '*Very* much friend. I'll stay. Go on then, get up the tree.'

Tin Win wouldn't have it. 'Char Lee go *too,*' he said in

the same fierce hiss. 'All go. Tin Win climb tree and follow. *Go!*' Tin Win was absolute boss of this operation and they all knew it and went obediently, straggling behind the main party as much as they dared.

'What a fantastic kid that is,' said Charlie. 'He's onto something, isn't he?'

'I'd say so.'

'What?'

'Wait.'

The waiting time was short. Tin Win came running down the trail, his legs a brown blur of action against the sombre jungle background, and caught them up. 'Tin Win right,' he said to Charlie. 'Tin Win always very much right.'

'For God's sake, what is it?' asked Charlie.

'Tin Win see plane. See Dove. Crash.'

'Crashed?' said Charlie and Roz together in dismay.

'Small crash. Much small,' explained the problem boy reassuringly. 'Not hurt crash.'

Then two cataclysms happened together. Charlie Thompson erupted into instant, violent anger, and Ma Hla came walking back to find them. 'You have trouble here?' she asked softly. 'Ma Hla give help?'

Charlie seemed to grow two feet or more as he stepped towards the tiny woman and towered over her. 'Who in hell d'you think you're crossing, you little creep?' he shouted. 'The Dove's through there! You know it's through there. Bergman's through there. Jonno's through there. So what's it all about, come on, give with the explanations.' He reached out to grab her slender arm but she ducked aside, unslung her rifle and cocked it. The problem boy drifted away to mingle with the other boys meandering back towards the river.

'Have seen Dove?' said Ma Hla still softly, but with studied coldness and nodding her head.

Charlie drew breath to shout again, then Perry cut in, covering for Tin Win. 'Darn right we've seen it,' he said. 'Go ahead, Ma Hla. Let's hear from you.' But Charlie didn't wait.

'Do what you like with that popgun,' he yelled, 'but we're going through now, *now* – just keep out of the way. Let's go, Perry.' He swung to move off along the trail. Ma Hla fired a single shot which had enormous sound, stunningly loud and sharpened by the confinement of the trees. Charlie's face, already red, went redder from shock, and he stopped and turned, confronting her. 'Put that thing down,' he said in anger that had gone quiet and was the more impressive for being so. Ma Hla, holding the little carbine at hip level, moved the foresight to point towards Charlie's glistening forehead, and kept her finger on the trigger. She called out something in the language the boys understood, and they all removed the pistols from their waistbands and held them at readiness. The little woman had assumed command of her army.

Soon after the sound of the shot, Clyne came hurrying towards them all, his face raised and anxious, scanning ahead. 'Say, what's the trouble here? I heard a...' He stopped talking and walking, and for a second or two, simply stared. 'Ma Hla, my dear ... what, I mean, in heaven's name! Please, whatever's happening here, please, put the gun down – these are our guests.'

She looked at him indifferently and said something to two of the boys who turned their pistols deliberately at Clyne, keeping their eyes down, but doing as they were told. Clyne seemed to have gone mentally numb and was swallowing air like a man afraid he might suffocate.

Moving a step or two closer he managed to say, 'My dear, I think ... I think you must be ill.' He tilted his head down to peer at Charlie, Perry and Roz, grouped together now and tensely watchful of everything going on. 'I do apologise, Perry,' mumbled Clyne. 'Yes, to all of you. I'm ah, more embarrassed than I can say. There's some extraordinary misunderstanding here. If you'll just keep calm I'm sure we can clear it up and get the guns put away. I'd like a private talk with my wife if, ah, you don't mind.' He switched to her again. 'Ma Hla, my dear, just come a few steps away with me – look, over there. Let's talk this over, the two of us.'

For a high calibre brain like Clyne it was a preposterous hope. Something had happened to Ma Hla. She was utterly changed and in no mood for sweet-cakes and a whisper in the bushes. 'Walt, join the other imperialists,' she said. Amazing how curt that singy little voice could be. She waved the carbine right to left and left to right two or three times in a gesture that could mean only one thing: move.

'What?' said Clyne.

'I say join the other imperialists, enemies of the people, all imperialists together. Cross river before dark, then talk. No talk on way – all silent.'

Charlie spotted Tin Win among a group of boys and hoped for a sign, a quick glance, smile, anything, but Tin Win had the same indifferent air as the other kids; it seemed as if Ma Hla could hypnotise them all, make them serve her will; he had the Nambu eight millimetre in his hand, the breechblock pulled back, ready for action. So the walk began in eerie silence broken by occasional jungle squawks, grunts and flappings, and the swish of machetes. By the time they reached the boat it was more than half dark and Perry, Roz and Charlie were being eaten alive by mosquitoes.

Ma Hla took all the proper precautions for the crossing. She sent Clyne first, guarded by four boys, then the others, one at a time and always with pistols waving about to ensure their good behaviour. Evidently she regarded Charlie as the greatest danger and she took him last with the carbine ready for action, and two boys to haul the boat across.

They found the Land-Rovers just before the full darkness of night had set in and turned on an assortment of lights. Ma Hla thumped the trailer's side with the stock of her carbine. 'All sit in trailer,' she ordered. 'Not leave trailer until Ma Hla say.' Clyne beckoned the others in, then turned wearily for another attempt at a word with his wife.

'We've done so much together,' he said, 'achieved so much. Can't you at least explain?'

All Ma Hla's femininity and poise vanished then and she began a long, hectoring speech full of hate and hysteria. 'Joe Bergman American,' she shouted. 'Joe Bergman enemy of Namkai people, fight for imperialist exploitation. Ma Hla fight other way, for People's Liberation Congress, for unification of the great peasant state of Namkai...' The speech went on for an age. Phrases recurred and recurred. 'Exploitation ... solidarity ... final victory ... imperialism ... super-traitors ... capitalist roaders ... monsters, demons and the dregs of society ...' She finished with a special attack on Bergman. 'You think Joe Bergman my friend? Not friend, Ma Hla's enemy. Enemy of Namkai people.' Then, with a downward curve of her small mouth she added, 'Joe Bergman agent for CIA. Spy, traitor. I spend years watching him.'

By this time Clyne was sitting on the rear edge of the trailer, the tailboard lowered. 'Ma Hla,' he said. 'Joe isn't even American, he's English.' She looked as if she might start another rave, but Clyne hadn't quite finished. 'So, Ma Hla, for me, our family, there is nothing – no feeling?' She looked at him for a moment, then turned and walked away, leaving two armed boys to guard the trailer. Soon she called a meeting of her army; the boys gathered round her and she gave them a long lecture. After that there was much activity. The tarpaulin top was fixed over the trailer leaving one end open, where the young guards stood or sat; also, a bright light was brought up and placed inside the tailboard, illuminating the prisoners and attracting vast numbers of insects that hummed, whirred, buzzed and collided.

Such talk as there was came in bursts spaced out by long pauses. They were all sitting close to each other near the front of the trailer, as far from the invading insects as possible. Early on, Charlie said, 'I'm going to get out of here if it's the last thing I do.'

'Yeah?' murmured Perry. 'Take a look at Ma Hla's face. It probably *will* be the last thing you do.' Then he turned to Clyne. 'What about it, Walt? Any ideas?'

'No, no. I haven't.'

'This must have been a bad shock for you.'

'Yes, a shock.'

'I know how you must be feeling. I'm sorry.'

Clyne shrugged. 'In the east you never know, never know. You must be accepting, fatalistic.'

They could see a cooking party at work in the distance – flames came from portable stoves and a wood fire. Ma Hla was flitting about keeping it all controlled. For a while they just watched.

'Walt,' said Perry softly, 'she's going to attack Joe in the morning, isn't she? I mean, what else?'

'That could be so.'

'But Joe's got a lot of fire power himself.'

'I guess he has.'

Charlie cut in, a good deal less softly. 'What's more, he's got Jonno. By God we've got to do something!' Roz squeezed his hand, and there was another silence. After a while, Ma Hla appeared at the other end of the trailer and looked inside, apparently checking; she had the carbine slung from her right shoulder as usual. Roz threw her an appealing look, hoping for some woman-to-woman response, but nothing happened. Ma Hla ignored her husband, too, and seemed about to go when Perry spoke her name.

'Ma Hla.'

She stood, listening, her eyes glittering in the yellow light.

'You're figuring you'll attack Joe in the morning – I'd think that's a good assumption. Now look. You've got a carbine there – I'd say it's the old M1 with fifteen rounds in the magazine and, okay, you've got maybe thirty seconds to do a little damage with that. Then you've got the kids with the old eight millimetre Nambus – but you couldn't knock a hole through a piece of paper with those. Now think about Joe. He's got a whole arms dump out there, you said. *And* he knows what to do with it. Ma Hla, you're going to lose this fight. Now let's show we've got brains, let's go for talking instead of shooting. We can work out a deal.'

The little mouth went into its downward curve again. 'You think Ma Hla a fool? Ma Hla not fool. Send two boys from farm for help from glorious comrades. Boys use motorbike, travel quick. Comrades soon here. We wait.' She changed the guard boys for two others and walked away.

Perry looked at Clyne. 'Do you believe all that?' he asked.

'Afraid I do.'

Charlie hunched forward, both fists clenched. 'Okay,' he said, 'here's the forecast. In the morning the glorious comrades come, they take Bergman and Jonno by surprise, lob the high explosive in and open up the rapid fire, and that means they're dead – Jonno dead! Then they come for us. Right? So what do we do? I'll tell you what. We bust out of here right now and take our chances. It can't get better, only worse, so let's go.'

He'd raised his voice a bit too much and the boy guards came closer, the Nambus ready. 'Er, those guns,' muttered Perry. 'Despite what I said, they'll kill you, and don't doubt it. Just sit quiet a moment, let this blow over.'

So they sat in silence as more of the night slipped away. They were given a small portion each of fish and rice, and water to drink. Roz nodded off, her head against Perry's shoulder. Several times Charlie seemed about to say something but held the words back, and clenched and unclenched his fists. Mentally, Clyne no longer seemed to be with them at all, his face had gone blank, like the face of a man in a coma. The insects kept up their futile night manoeuvres by the lamp, many of them now lying helpless, wrong way up and waggling spindly legs.

Charlie heard a scratching sound at the front of the trailer and turned, apprehensively, to investigate. It sounded like the scratchings of a rat on the prowl. The noise came from a point where the canvas cover was tied down to the body of the trailer, and as he studied it, a small brown index finger came up through the join like a tiny flag. Then came a whisper. 'If Char Lee hear Tin Win make bang bang. Char Lee not speak, not word, not big bang bang. Go make not big bang bang.' Charlie gulped and knocked the wooden front of the trailer with his elbow twice, close to the little finger.

'Tin Win get Jon No, Joe Bergman, bring here.' The finger disappeared.

A whirl of emotions swept through Charlie. He wanted to plead with Tin Win to be careful, wanted desperately to go with him, felt humbled by the bravery of this small peasant boy, and was overrun by hope, fear, affection and impatience. His face muscles worked with the stress of it all and Perry, who hadn't been able to make out the whisperings, leaned forward. 'What's going on, Charlie?' he asked in a side of the mouth murmur.

'It's fantastic, Perry,' whispered Charlie. 'Fantastic! Tin Win – he's on his way to get them, Jonno and Joe. He just told me, and now he's gone – alone. What an incredible kid! Well I hope he's all right.'

'Me too. Ssh, let's keep quiet.'

'But what when they get here?'

'Ssh. Wait.' Wait – always a thing Charlie found difficult to do.

Jonathan woke to feel himself being shaken by the shoulder. It was still dark, still cold, they were still at the crashed Dove locked in the jungle; so it was still real and not an appalling dream. He looked up into the face of Bergman. 'Where've you put my medicine, you little beggar?' the man was asking. Jonno sat up, remembered instantly, and wondered what the penalty would be; best to get on with facing it.

'I tipped all the bottles away. The whisky's all gone.'

Bergman gaped at him in disbelief. 'You wouldn't have the nerve,' he said. 'Go on – where's my holdall?'

'Round by the front of the aircraft – and the bottles are empty.'

Bergman walked off in search. 'You little brat,' he said. 'If they are I'll give you the hiding of a lifetime. One part of your anatomy won't be cold.'

Jonno sat waiting apprehensively. At least the man was more or less sober – and he was going to have to stay that way from now on, no doubt there. It was a long time, two or three minutes, until Bergman came back, and Jonno braced for the action. But nothing happened. Bergman stood for a moment looking down at the boy, then just crouched beside him. 'Why don't we sit in the Dove?' he asked.

'You said there was a dangerous snake in there.'

'I did? Is there?'

'Well, blimey, I don't know!'

'Maybe we'll stay out here. We'll look inside when it's light.' He made himself more comfortable, then groaned.

Jonathan looked at him through the not quite total darkness. 'What's wrong?'

'Only my head. I know, I know – you don't have to sympathise.'

On the whole it seemed to Jonno that the conversation was going along very well – much better than expected. 'Joe,' he said tentatively, 'can we start back to the farm in the morning?'

Bergman took a while to reply, then said, 'You know, those North Namkais had more than a hundred thousand men down in the south. And they didn't wear uniforms, a lot of them didn't; no, they'd come on through as anything, women, monks, peasant farmers. Take a look at them and they'd be planting rice; look away and, hell, they'd shoot you in the back.'

'Joe!' Desperation was having its effect on Jonno's voice. 'Can't you forget all that? It's *over*.'

'Yeah? I had a buddy, Bob Parker, Eighty-Second Airborne Division. Nice fella, I liked Bob. They caught him, skinned him alive, just left his face so we'd know him in the morning. And old Bob used to say he was born lucky – think of it! Well, his luck ran out one Tuesday night. That's what they did to Bob.'

'Joe, please ... You're hopeless,' Jonno said despairingly. 'All locked up in the past. Hopeless.' He was in the act of lowering his forehead onto his knee when a sudden movement to the right set him rigid with terror, heart pounding; but a very brief terror. The moving thing was Tin Win, now crouched beside him, smiling.

'Tin Win come. Take Jon No, Joe Bergman back. Take guns. Ma Hla bad woman. Tin Win know for long time, always right.'

Jonathan went momentarily wild with joy. He flung his arms round Tin Win's shoulders and the two boys embraced each other, rocking with laughter. But Jonno's laugh was more and also less than laughter, a surge of feeling close to hysteria, and he knew it, in a moment fighting to avoid tears from the abrupt release of tension. He broke free of Tin Win's arms and stood up, leaning his face against the cold surface of Oscar India's fuselage, shaking as if a jungle fever had him.

'Well, I'll be damned,' said Bergman laconically, recognising Tin Win's dim outline. 'The problem boy! How the hell did you get here?'

'Ma Hla through trees, Joe. Bad Woman. Take others prisoner. Send for comrades, People's Liberation Congress army, she one. Ma Hla want you dead.'

The whites of Tin Win's eyes shone like little flashlights through the darkness. Jonathan looked down to see Bergman staring at them, leaning forward like a floored fighter about to leap to his feet.

'Tin Win tell truth,' the problem boy went on. 'Always truth. Ma Hla want you dead.'

'I believe you, Tin Win,' Bergman said at last, easing back. 'Fact is I did have moments when I wondered, just wondered – but I put those doubts aside. Funny how you can do that. The bitch.'

'Joe drink too much, not think. Tin Win think. Bring

boat for Joe, Jon No. Lead way back before light. Take guns, we go now. Tin Win for Joe.'

Bergman leaned past Jonno and waggled Tin Win's knee. 'Thanks, Tin Win,' he said. 'You're my friend – I've always known that, and I'm truly grateful. But look – I'm not coming. Take Jonno, get him back safely. I'll wait here for those stooks, and oh boy, will I be ready for them! See, I still have my settlement to make.'

'Ma Hla's people kill Joe,' said Tin Win earnestly.

'Maybe, maybe not.' Bergman ran the thin fingers through his silver hair again, the characteristic gesture. 'But I'll lay a little bet: if they do, I betcha I take at least a dozen of 'em with me.' Tin Win stared through the darkness, trying to understand.

For Jonathan it was different. He'd only known Bergman a day or two, but there wasn't another living person who'd come so close to this obsessed man's soul. He tried to explain. 'Joe means what he says. He won't come – I know because we've talked a lot.' Tin Win looked up into the other boy's face and still didn't understand. 'You see, he's ... well, Joe feels ... I don't think I can explain, but he won't come.'

Bergman stood up. 'We ought to get moving,' he said. 'I'll catch them coming over the river – hope they can swim.' He laughed derisively. 'I've got a seven-six-two self-loader and two old Stens – they'll do for starters. I want the ammo boxes and all the grenades, ah yes, and my little mortar. Look, you guys, help me carry the stuff down to the river, then I'll watch you across.'

They hurried to the camouflaged shed where Bergman buckled a belt and holster round his waist. He pulled out an all black gun, examined it, and dropped it back into the holster, looking content. 'A Luger,' he said. 'Your very good friend when the action gets close. Now, let's load up.' They carried out heavy wooden crates and the guns, a two-inch mortar., assorted knives, and a pick and a spade, stacking them onto a rubber-tyred trolley and after a brief rest staggered towards the river, pulling and pushing, the sweat soon flowing. When they were still a longish way from the river, the trolley couldn't be manoeuvred any further through the thickening trees and undergrowth. 'Right boys,' gasped Bergman. 'From here it's shanks's pony. Get the stuff off.'

By the time they'd unloaded and pushed through to dump the crates and guns where Bergman wanted them, Jonno was dizzy from exhaustion and hunger. He leaned against a tree watching Bergman dig himself in behind slightly raised ground; a good ridge position with commanding views of half a mile or so of river, both to right and left. Weird and dreadful to think of the drama due to happen here; blood leading into the black water, screams, lives ending.

Then Tin Win spoke, and brought him back to the present. 'Joe come,' he said in an oddly frail voice. 'Tin Win need Joe.' Jonathan felt suddenly sorry for the small brown boy with the white eyes flashing in the dark, the boy who'd always seemed so sure but who needed his 'father'.

Bergman, crouched to take sighting views of the river, looked up, then stood up and put an arm round Tin Win's shoulders. 'Tin Win manage very well,' he said gently. 'Tin Win clever boy and good boy. Tin Win president of Burma someday.' It finished there. Bergman went back to his preparations while Tin Win stood, silently staring at the ground.

Jonathan tried to help. 'I wish you would come, Joe,' he said. 'All you have to do is change your mind. Why wait here to be killed?'

The man paused from his work again. 'It isn't written on stone that I've got to be killed. But if I am it doesn't matter. See, I've been afraid of plenty of things but I'm not afraid of death. Does that sound strange?'

'A bit.'

'Well, it's true. Now listen, you two better paddle across that river.'

The suggestion brought new and anxious thoughts to Jonathan. 'What do we do when we get to Ma Hla?' he asked. 'She'll take us prisoner like the others, won't she? Maybe worse.'

Bergman considered the question for a moment. 'No,' he said presently, 'she won't. You won't let her – here's what you do. First, if Ma Hla's carrying a gun, get it away from her. Don't ask me how but, Tin Win, you do it some way while Jonno keeps out of sight. Remember she's not expecting trouble which is a hell of an advantage to you. Then, Jonno, you cover Ma Hla while Tin Win tells the boys I've appointed him leader. Bingo! It's all over, done. They'll follow anyone who's strong. So, Tin Win, be strong. And remind them I'm their father – I brought them out from the guns. Now, let's find the boat and get you two away. I've still got a lot to do.'

For most of the way they walked in silence, then Tin Win said, 'Bring little boat across river for Joe.'

'Okay, thanks. But hurry.'

Bergman helped them float the bigger boat from the spot where Tin Win had struggled single-handed to beach it, and the two boys scrambled in. When they turned to say good-bye, Bergman had already started back; a thin shadowy figure hunching towards his private war. Jonathan's eyes went wet at so sudden and bleak a parting, and he carefully turned away from Tin Win beginning the long paddle eastward. Three crossings had to be made to fetch the little boat, carry it over then go off again to the far bank. They toiled at the paddles. When they dumped the little boat for Bergman they looked hopefully for the man, and Jonno softly called his name. He didn't appear.

Dawn had put a silver edging to the horizon when they arrived back at the makeshift camp. The two boys hid behind a giant tree and sized up the scene before them. Several farm boys were asleep on groundsheets, the prisoners were evidently still in the guarded trailer and Ma Hla was catnapping, sitting at the foot of a central tree and leaning against it; her carbine was across her lap, a portable lamp nearby. 'We be quick,' whispered Tin Win. 'Light come.'

Jonathan, tired enough to fall down, nodded. 'Take gun.' Tin Win was handing him the Nambu. 'Take quick.' Jonathan took it, and felt the warmth of the metal from contact with Tin Win's stomach. 'Tin Win go, take gun from Ma Hla. Then Jon No come very quick with Nambu. Tin Win talk to boys. Tin Win is leader. Jon No is second leader. Tin Win go.'

Before Jonathan could begin to reply Tin Win had gone, unarmed and heading right into the heart of the danger. This was the peak moment, with success or disaster a second or two away. Jonno reacted with more heavy heartbeats as fright took over again; but fear brought the benefit, important at present, of ending the numbing weariness; energy surged through his system. He watched.

Tin Win approached with the stealth of a panther, tracking in behind Ma Hla's tree in the line of shadow cast where it blocked the light from the lamp. The little woman didn't move. At the tree, close now to Ma Hla, he waited for what seemed an age to Jonathan standing on the outskirts of the action, the hair on the nape of his neck standing up and the blood pounding through his head.

At last Tin Win came round the tree, snatched the carbine from Ma Hla's lap and began a terrible shouting. Jonathan sprang into action, waving the Nambu and running towards the centre of the camp. Farm boys popped up on their groundsheets, rubbing their eyes, others, on guard duty, stared across, some reaching uncertainly for their pistols.

Jonathan arrived at Tin Win's side not knowing what to say or where to point the gun, but he was there and it helped. Ma Hla stood, knees bent and back arched, staring at Tin Win with her hands towards him, fingers extended like a strangler's. Tin Win clung to the carbine and backed away a step or two, still shouting. Other boys were approaching now, in obvious amazement and uncertainty. One of them drew his Nambu and raised it towards Tin Win. It was Jonno's moment, and he responded. 'No you don't!' he yelled over Tin Win's screeching, and took aim at the boy – who lowered the gun but kept it in his hand.

Ma Hla showed signs of recovering from the shock she had suffered and began calling chosen boys by name. Jonathan sensed with alarm that the finish of this was by no means sure; the woman was making a come-back, overpowering little Tin Win with her anger and practised leadership. 'Fire the gun,' Jonathan hissed. 'Not to kill anyone, just put it to your shoulder and *fire*!' Still screaming propaganda, Tin Win positioned the carbine and squeezed the trigger. Three or four shots crashed out, and the recoil sent him staggering. But the effect on Ma

Hla was good. The bullets smashed into the tree close to her, one richocheting off and whining its way through space, and she jumped visibly, took several quick steps rearwards – and lost the point. Then a great bellowing of laughter carried across, and Charlie was out of the trailer pointing derisively at Ma Hla and rocking about. Several onlooking boys began to smile too, and suddenly Jonathan knew with wild happiness that they had won.

Behind Charlie came Perry, and behind him, Roz, looking strained at first but then laughing too, from relief. You could see Clyne's bald head glinting from the trailer but he didn't get out.

Charlie strode up to Ma Hla, unimpressed by her catlike stance and smouldering anger. 'Jonno,' he said, 'hi there – fantastic to see you. Wonderful.'

Jonathan gave him a jerky smile. 'God, Charlie, I can't believe I'm back.' After the words came a sudden shudder, and Charlie roughed up his hair.

'You seem to be all in one piece still, Captain. Very well done, both of you. We've got a lot to talk about, but later. Right now keep that woman covered and don't let her get too close.' He turned to focus contempt and anger on her. 'Look, Ma Hla, you've lost. Got that? You're finished. Be sensible so we don't have to shoot you.'

Then Perry came up to Tin Win, who had stopped the shouted speech and was beckoning the boys to gather round. 'Hell of a nice performance, Tin Win,' Perry said. 'And what was all the shouting about?'

Tin Win grinned hugely. 'I say Tin Win your leader. Joe Bergman say so. Ma Hla bad woman. Joe Bergman your father. Follow Tin Win.'

'Follow Tin Win – pretty goddam good advice that,' said Perry. 'It'll do for me. Can I make a suggestion, Leader?' Tin Win nodded, still smiling. 'I think you should call in the guns, or most of them anyway. You and Jonno keep yours, give Charlie and me one and maybe a couple of the boys you can really trust. For the rest – let's stack 'em on the trailer.'

The problem boy leader agreed.

8 Battle

As the morning sun rose against a pale clear sky, the camp was very changed. Jonno and Tin Win slept side by side on groundsheets, Roz watching them attentively, flicking at insects that might disturb this short and vital rest. Nearby, Charlie had a breakfast party organised, frying the usual eggs and rice, and brewing an immense can of tea.

Clyne perched at the rear of the trailer, his legs dangling out. Close to him on the ground, sitting upright and still, like a figure of wax, was his wife. He'd made a number of efforts to talk, but Ma Hla had ignored him utterly, and they sat now in a strained communion of silence, two farm boys with them on guard.

When breakfast arrived, Roz woke Jonno and Tin Win who both flopped about, heavy and helpless with sleepiness, until hunger got them fully going. They'd had almost two hours on the groundsheets – enough to make a difference; they ate fast. Clyne took one egg and a spoonful of rice, but Ma Hla refused even to look at food.

After breakfast Charlie asked Jonno to tell of his night with Bergman. 'Don't leave anything out,' he said. 'Give us the whole works.'

Jonathan did; he began slowly, describing the terrible moment of take-off at the farm, then speeded up, his eyes wide as in the telling he relived the bombs, the crash, the horrors of the long dark hours with Bergman and, finally, the utter joy of finding Tin Win there for him. Afterwards Charlie came over and crouched beside him. 'That was really something to go through, Jonno,' he said. 'Well done, Captain.' The others agreed and murmured congratulations to Jonno and Tin Win.

Next they moved on to the subject of future plans. What now? Perry said, 'I guess we head back to the farm – but what about her?' He gestured at Ma Hla.

'And what about Joe?' added Roz.

Charlie faced her. 'There's nothing to be done for Joe,' he said bluntly, 'so let's get the hell out of here. I don't know about her. Maybe we just leave the silly cow here.'

'No,' It was Roz, and she shook her head disapprovingly. 'We don't abandon Ma Hla like that.'

'No? And what d'you think she'd do for you?'

'That isn't the point – is it?'

Clyne had almost nothing to say but gave vague little nods now and then to show he was listening. They were still undecided when an engine revved in the distance, a faint but unmistakable sound; Ma Hla turned towards it, a hint of a smile on her lips. 'That's them,' said Charlie. 'The lovely lads of the PLC on another glorious mission; more throats to cut.' They paused while the revving came closer, and suddenly Charlie grinned. 'Someone's got a heavy foot there,' he added. 'I think your friends have got problems, Ma Hla – the united anti-imperialist jeeps are getting stuck in the jolly old trees. Great.'

They could pick out several engines now, probably three, and struggling. Ma Hla began to quiver with emotion, and Jonno felt a new sweep of alarm. 'What if they attack us?' he asked.

Before anyone answered, Clyne made his first real contribution to the meeting. He had sad eyes levelled at the little woman. 'Go to them, Ma Hla,' he said quietly but with strength. 'Join your people. Go.'

Ma Hla turned to look at him, the first time she'd done

so since midnight, held the look for a while, glanced at the others and, still quivering, stood up. But then she paused, confronting them, rigid and arched, the black eyes narrowed in suspicion.

Clyne spoke again. 'No trap, Ma Hla. Just go.' Then, to Charlie, he added, 'Give her the carbine.'

'Yeah? And have us all shot?' Charlie tugged at the reddish ragged hair on his left lip. 'Have you gone out of your mind?'

'Please do as I say, Charlie, give her the gun. She won't shoot us, I give you my word. And see, she might need protection.'

'Darn right she might. And what if she opens up on Joe – your pal remember.'

'*Give her the gun!*' Clyne had that assertive air that just occasionally took over from the more usual dreaminess.

'Do as Walt says, Charlie.' It was Perry, the quiet drawly voice loaded with authority. 'Give her the gun.'

Charlie tugged on for a little while then threw it across, the muzzle pointing skyward, and Clyne grabbed the stock awkwardly, lurching sideways to do so. He stepped to Ma Hla and handed her the carbine. 'Take it,' he said. 'Don't use it on Joe. And go.'

She walked the first few paces, turning her head from time to time watchfully, then suddenly broke into a wild run, calling out in frenzy and disappearing through the trees. Roz gazed after her. 'What an ugly scene,' she said. 'Unbelievable.'

Jonno came anxiously back to thoughts of the PLC and its menacing advance. 'What if they come belting through here?' he said. 'They'll shoot us, won't they? Listen, they're close.' Fear was catching at his voice.

'What d'you think, Walt?' asked Perry. 'Jonno's right

you know, they're closing in on us. Should we lose ourselves in the trees?'

Clyne shook his shiny head. 'They're not looking for us. Don't worry.'

'Meaning they'll head straight down for Joe?'

'Yes. They've got no right here in Burma, so they won't want to hang about.' This was the other Clyne, the strong one showing again, and they believed him.

'Okay,' said Charlie. 'That's that. Let's push off home – I'm tired of trees.'

Perry didn't agree. 'No point in actually advertising that we're here,' he insisted. 'If the PLC hear engines they could get curious, so just hold it a minute. We might as well sit down.' They sat or squatted, the farm boys in one group near the trailer, the others, with Tin Win, more on the edge of the camp. Charlie came beside Jonno, tapped him on the knee and grinned reassuringly. The boy was not at ease.

Soon the revving quietened and the shouting stopped. 'Ma Hla joining them maybe,' wondered Perry aloud. 'Would you say so, Walt?'

The bald head nodded. 'I guess so, I guess so.'

'Well, they haven't shot her.'

The motors began their frenzied revving again for a while, then stopped, and a heavy silence shrouded the jungle. 'They've left the trucks,' said Clyne, who seemed to know everything. 'Now for the kill. They're moving in on Joe.'

Jonno shuddered, and Tin Win – who'd been very quiet – scrambled to his feet. 'I go,' he said. 'Help Joe.' The problem boy began to run past Charlie who grabbed his hand and jerked him to a stop.

'It's no good, Tin Win,' he said. 'There's nothing you can do. Come on, sit down again.' Slowly the boy sat, and

Charlie held on to the hand until he was sure of him.

'How many?' murmured Perry. 'Fifteen? Twenty?'

'I guess about that,' confirmed Clyne.

'Real heroes, eh? Twenty to one.'

Roz had a hand over her eyes. 'It's a nightmare,' she said. 'Horrible. We ... we just sit and wait.' Charlie looked again and again at his watch as if he didn't believe the reading. There was no more talk.

Then, very suddenly, ferocious shooting began from the direction of the river, then screams and shouts, then a mix up of rifle and machine gun fire, then two heavy crashes and more frantic shouting. Jonno hugged his own shoulders and lowered his head.

Twice the battle seemed to have ended, later to flare erratically into life with more exchanges of fire and the heavy crump of grenades or mortar shells. When the third quiet came, it remained. 'I reckon that's the end,' said Perry at last.

'Sixteen minutes he kept going,' added Charlie. 'Wonder how many he took.'

In a while the jeep engines started with more of the random revving. Perry stood slowly up, looking towards the sound. 'He didn't get them all, then,' he said. 'Pity.'

'Not all,' agreed Charlie. 'But I bet he's done okay. Let's go and see. Tin Win, tell the other kids to stay here, you come with us.' By now there was no doubt about Tin Win's status as boss among his friends. He gathered the boys together, shouted instructions in his reedy voice, then came stalking back.

'Boys stay, guard camp,' he said. They waited for the jeep engines to fade from hearing, then picked their way through the trees again along last night's trail. Jonathan glimpsed a shape before the others and stood, pointing.

'Look,' he called out. There, in among the trees where

they thickened on the downslope towards the river, was a crudely built, jeep-like truck.

'Chinese,' said Clyne. 'Their idea of a jeep.'

'Quiet everybody,' whispered Perry. 'Some of those soldiers may still be around.' They waited for several minutes watching, then crept soundlessly forward to the truck, taking cover all the way behind trees. There were no soldiers to be seen. The truck seemed undamaged, and after they'd looked all round it – including underneath and at the engine for booby traps – Charlie climbed in and turned the starter key. At once the engine fired and he let it run for a while, then switched off.

It all seemed odd to Jonathan. 'Why would they leave that behind?' he asked. 'A perfectly good truck.'

'I can think of one possible reason,' said Perry. 'Maybe there were just so darn few soldiers left, there was nobody to drive it.'

'Blimey. That could be it, couldn't it? *Blimey!*'

They pushed on down the trail and arrived at the edge of the Salween. Except for a low hiss from the swiftly flowing water, silence had come to the battle scene. There were no signs of life – only of death. Out near the middle of the river were shredded remains of the dinghy still hanging from the tightly stretched line. On the far bank they saw four bodies sprawled in ugly attitudes. Jonathan stared at them morbidly until Perry spoke. 'Where was Bergman then?'

'There, by that hump.' Jonathan showed him. 'You can see just about everything from there,' he added. 'A brilliant spot to choose. He had to dig himself in a bit.'

On their own side of the river were curious scars in the ground where jungle grass had been thrown up and saplings uprooted. 'Crikey, there's been a battle or something here, too,' said Jonno, surprised.

'Mortar bombs,' suggested Charlie. 'Must be. Old Joe there was a real one-man army. Bet those creeps were surprised.'

'Poor things,' said Roz. 'I think I'm sorry for them, too. All this killing – and for what? Come away everybody, please.' They did move further away keeping close to the water's edge. Jonathan kept looking across at Bergman's ridge, imagining him crouched there, blasting away at the soldiers he hated so much.

'How many *do* you reckon he got?' he asked Perry.

'Well, there are four over there for sure. And I guess there's a boatload keeping the fish company a long way down river by now – so I'd say a minimum of nine. Probably more.'

'He wanted a dozen – he said that. Can we get over there somehow? I mean we must know if . . . if Joe's there, mustn't we?'

Perry shrugged. 'We've got no boat left.'

'But he might be there. Might not even be dead, just wounded.'

'Jonno, listen, if he's there – which I very much doubt – he's dead; the PLC would make sure of that, believe me; they're not exactly chivalrous on the battlefield, remember. It's better not to go.'

Tin Win had been slowly walking away from them towards the river. He made a sudden dash for the taut line and began to haul himself along it, his legs splashing through the water. Charlie ran after him, waving and shouting. 'Come back – what d'you think you're doing, you idiot.' But Tin Win's brown torso bobbed its way towards the other bank, and he didn't look round. 'God knows what's in that river,' said Charlie. 'He'll be eaten alive.'

'That kid . . .' muttered Perry wagging his head. 'Some

cool customer, eh? Really, he just doesn't know what it is to feel afraid. I've never met anyone like him.'

'Nor me,' said Jonathan sounding uncharacteristically humble – and Charlie glanced across at him and smiled.

They followed Tin Win's painfully slow and jerky journey, and saw him pull himself safely onto the far bank. 'Hell's bells, I feel I want to cheer,' said Charlie. Tin Win's small figure went slowly up the bank to the ridge, then he dropped out of sight where Bergman had been. The others waited, watching. Minutes passed and the tension grew. 'What the heck is he up to?' Charlie asked, a frown lining his sun-reddened brow.

At last Tin Win reappeared and walked down towards the river. But when they expected him to splash into the water again. he didn't; he just sat on the bank, motionless. Charlie cupped his big hands and bawled at him to come back. 'You big dodo,' said Perry. 'He'll never hear you against the river. He's just taking his time. Leave him.'

'I think I know what it is,' Roz said quietly. 'It's sort of a little ceremony. He's missing Joe, poor kid.'

'It's funny, but I miss Joe too.' The words were Jonno's, his bright face changed by seriousness. 'I hated him at times – you know when we were stuck out there by the Dove. Yet, well, when you've gone through all that with someone . . .'

'You don't have to explain,' muttered Perry.

'He could be really nice when he wanted to.'

'I know. He was okay. Clyne thinks so, too. Look at him.' They looked. Clyne had wandered a way upstream, alone; he'd slipped out again to his private world of the mind. 'Poor old Clyne,' Perry went on. 'Bergman and Ma Hla, both gone.'

Eventually Tin Win rose, turned slowly the whole way

round, perhaps locking the memory of the scene in his mind for ever, then plunged back into the greyness of the river. New anxiety took hold of the group on the home bank, waiting and hoping. Then, as he came closer, Charlie waded out waist deep to meet him, a strong arm stretched out towards the boy. They met in the river and finished together, Charlie awkwardly holding the rope with one hand and Tin Win's elbow with the other. At the bank's edge, Charlie heaved the boy up, draped him over his shoulder and climbed the slope, water streaming from his trousers. Perry, Jonno and Roz scrambled towards them to help.

At a patch of grass clear of the shade of trees, Charlie gently lowered Tin Win and stretched him out to recover. The boy was shivering uncontrollably, his teeth clattering like tiny hammers. 'He's frozen through,' said Charlie, wrenching his shirt off and using the dry part of it to rub Tin Win down. 'Come on, Perry let's have yours next. I'm telling you, that's the coldest bit of water this side of the Arctic Ocean.' Perry threw his shirt across and Charlie carried on with the drying operations, rubbing hard back and front to stir up Tin Win's circulation. 'Apart from your pants you're dry now,' he said, throwing Perry's shirt back. 'How d'you feel?'

'T ... Tin Win st ... still c ... cold,' stuttered Tin Win.

'Yeah. It's got right into you, hasn't it? Jonno, switch shorts with Tin Win.'

'What? You'll be lucky,' answered Jonathan.

'Go on. You can dry them off better than he can. Just do it.'

'Well, blimey! *Blimey!*' The undisguised indignation followed them.

Standing by the hiss of the Salween, the sense of amusement ceased. There were the bodies to look at and, of course, Bergman's silent outpost – and Clyne, gauntly alone with his thoughts. It had been a very nasty affair.

In less than half an hour Tin Win was fully recovered but silent. Charlie made two attempts to get him to talk and both times Tin Win pointedly turned away. Then Jonno had a try. 'I'm sorry about Joe, like you,' he said. 'Only I know it's much worse for you. Was ... was Joe there? I mean dead.'

'Joe not dead,' said Tin Win fiercely. '*Not* dead.'

'No?'

'*No!*'

Out of Tin Win's line of sight, Perry lifted a finger to his lips for silence. The adults – still without Clyne – stood listening intently as the two boys spoke.

'But how d'you know?' asked Jonathan. 'Did you, sort of see him or, well, what?'

Tin Win glanced at Jonno scornfully. 'Joe gone. And little boat gone. Joe fight soldiers then go away in boat. Tin Win clever and know, president of Burma some day. And Joe come back some day. Joe came back. Tin Win sure.'

Perry came forward now and gently pulled the hair on the nape of Tin Win's neck. 'That's nice to hear, Tin Win,' he said. 'And until he does, you help Walt run the farm – and, Jeeze, is he going to need you! Okay, everybody, let's leave it like that and get moving.' Yet again they trekked along the hot, moist trail.

It took less than an hour to break camp, but the bustle seemed to help Clyne come back to the real world. Roz and Peregrene joined him in his Land-Rover-trailer combination, leaving Charlie and Jonno to risk it with Tin Win. And, of course, Tin Win did insist on driving, and performed as badly as before. The first brutal start flung two farm boys half way out of the car's open back. Jonathan's turn to be scornful. 'Flip me, what a driver!' he said. 'Brilliant.' Tin Win seemed to take it as a compliment and battled on. After nearly two hours he flopped suddenly forward on the wheel – asleep. Charlie had been waiting for the moment, knocked the car out of gear and stopped it. He switched seats with the boy, settled him down and brought a drowsy Jonno in front too, squeezing him into the middle position. Both boys were sweating but deeply asleep when Charlie drove on.

They arrived at the farm in darkness, and staggered from the Land-Rovers and trailer exhausted. It had been a long, slow, rough journey with one stop for rice, eggs, tea and a rest on the way; except for Clyne, they went tottering quickly to bed, all decision left for the morning.

Clyne appeared to be freshest of them all. His comeback to reality was going well – he showed that by walking round the chicken house and returning pleased. 'Those hens are looking good,' he said to Perry. 'See, I've got them on automatic. They get fed and watered by time switches, and I've got temperature control – yep, and lights turn on to shorten the night. Puts egg production up between ten and fifteen per cent. It's been kind of experimental until now, but I guess we can say it's proved, eh?'

Peregrene yawned. 'Sure, Walt,' he said. 'That's great news. Good night.'

'Uhuh, good night. We'll have a get-together in the morning.'

Jonathan woke before Charlie and lay for a while enjoying the luxury of just being where he was; in a bed. His mind roamed over the previous day and the terrible night before it. And Tin Win! Heck, but that kid had guts – coming through the jungle alone in the dark, crossing the river, pinching Ma Hla's gun. Some kid. He looked at his right hand, unwashed and very grubby, and then at the neat sleeve of his pyjamas. There'd been no pyjama-style comforts in the jungle, only bugs and snakes and luminous eyes and the cold. He put the grubby hand back under the bedclothes. Really, they'd been lucky to get away with it, tramping about among all the cobras and tigers and things. Take those eyes in the night, when he'd moved away from Joe; they might easily have been a tiger's. Something to tell them about at school. Pity about Joe; he'd tried his best, just couldn't get him to come away . . .

Charlie snorted, then yawned noisily. 'Morning Captain,' he said.

'Hullo Charlie. You getting up, then?'

'Aah, soon.'

'Did I tell you how I threw Joe's whisky away?'

'You said you'd tipped it on the ground.'

'No, but earlier I told him I wanted a drink of the stuff, then threw the whole bottle away. I thought he would really clobber me.'

'If he'd had any sense he would've done.'

'I wish I'd been able to make him come with me. He'd still be alive. I should've found a way.'

Charlie propped himself up on an elbow and stared intently across at the boy. 'Listen, Jonno, you did a fantastic job and don't forget it. Don't quote me, but I'm actually proud of you. Fantastic job.'

'Tin Win did better.'

'No, he didn't. You both did brilliantly, you and Tin Win. You did what you had to do and it was darned tough, not one in a thousand kids could do it. So no comparisons.'

'I was scared stiff at times.'

'You think I'd have been different?'

'Thanks.'

Roz organized the breakfast routines, and Charlie and Perry helped. Jonno was sent by Clyne to the farm boys' hut for Tin Win. 'Tell him I'd like him to come here for breakfast,' Clyne had said.

It surprised Tin Win when Jonno walked in and passed on the message, but he came. They all sat down on the floor mats with more boiled eggs and tea before them. Clyne swirled his coconut milk round in a glass, examined it, sipped it, coughed lightly then spoke. 'We've had some terrible shocks,' he said, 'and I'd like to thank you all for what you've done. But, ah, there are two people here I want to say special thanks to, two young people.'

Jonathan looked up from his egg. *Young* people – there was danger here. Annoyingly, the man paused for several slow sips at this critical point, then at last resumed. 'Yes, I want to thank you Jonno, especially, for stopping Joe from dropping those bombs – and for the many other things you did when you were utterly alone. You are a very brave boy.'

'Hear, hear,' murmured Charlie nodding cheerful agreement – sending Jonathan red.

'And I want to thank *you*, Tin Win,' Clyne droned on. 'I want to thank you very much for saving Jonno and, well, for saving us all. You, too, are a very brave boy.'

Now it was Tin Win who nodded. 'Tin Win always brave boy,' he said blandly.

'Er, yes,' agreed Clyne, losing his way for a moment and finding more sips at the glass a useful diversion. He looked next at Peregrene. 'I guess it's all over, Perry,' he said. 'As you can see there'll be no flying here for a while, so I'm sure you want to get home. I'm sorry our plans went wrong. Thank you for coming, and for your support. And, of course, that goes for you, Roz, and, ah, Charlie.'

Perry smiled at him. 'It's been a rewarding experience for us, Walt, truly. Congratulations on all this' – he waved a hand through a quick rough circle – 'the farm is great, and it's good just to see this kind of nice thing happen. But you're right, there's really nothing left for us to do. Tell me, how do we get out of here?'

'I'll see the authorities in Kengtung today. The military will fly you to Rangoon, I'm almost certain, and you can connect with a Jumbo there for London. It shouldn't be a problem. Let me have your account before I go – the authorities can deal with that as well.'

'That's embarrassing. We haven't done anything.'

'We have,' said Charlie quickly. 'We've wrecked the Dove.'

Perry frowned, and spoke with a touch of coolness. 'Bad joke, Charlie. Walt, we'll settle for our expenses. But now, what about you when we go? You'll manage okay? Got any plans?'

The bald head wagged up and down. 'Oh sure, I'm going to ask Tin Win to move into the house with me for a start, to take Joe's place. Tin Win ...' he turned to the problem boy '... will you do that? Live here in the house?'

Tin Win didn't answer at first, and the situation was edging towards awkwardness. Then he came on with his usual directness. 'Tin Win live in house,' he said, 'until Joe back.'

'Right, right, of course,' babbled Clyne gratefully. 'When, ah, Joe returns we can have another think.'

Then Roz had a comment. 'There's one little problem, Walt. You'll be needing some feminine company round here, don't you think?'

To Jonathan's great interest, Clyne went pink not only in the face but on top of his head. 'Quite so, quite so,' he agreed. 'Well, there's a lady in Kengtung ... She's alone now. Daw Khin. I think it's possible she'll – well, I'll have to see.'

'Good lady,' said Tin Win unexpectedly. 'Daw Khin good wife for Walt.' Clyne's redness glowed brighter and brighter through the weathered skin, and he looked away.

'Walt!' Perry had a widening grin on his face. 'Man, but you're an operator – I'm telling you, the ladies had better watch out for Walt Clyne. Jeeze, what technique – another bird on his mind already!' He chuckled annoyingly on and on, and slapped his leg until Roz came quietly up to nudge him. Clyne, smiling bashfully, clearly didn't know where to look, and soon grabbed his glass and hurried with it from the room.

Next day an old army Dakota diverted to the farm and took them aboard. Clyne and his new partner, Tin Win, saw them out to the big tailwheeled aircraft and stood waving cheerfully as the heavy Pratt and Whitneys started up, the dust whirling out dramatically astern. It had been quite an easy parting, the disasters of a day or two before having already been coped with.

In the air they had to shout to be heard above the engine noise. 'Home in forty-eight hours or so,' yelled Charlie. 'Suits me.'

Then Perry had a thought that seemed to amuse him. 'He's done it, you know,' he bawled. 'Old Clyne, Daw Khin's moving in any time.'

'She is?' hollered Charlie. 'My God, he's a goer, that old boy. What with him and Tin Win! Astounding kid, Tin Win, isn't he?'

'Yeah, astounding.'

Jonathan scowled towards them. 'Tin Win's a rotten driver,' he yelled. 'And he can't fly aeroplanes at all.'

It made them all laugh, even – after a little pause for the scowl to fade – Jonathan himself.

Alexander Barrie

Fly for Three Lives 45p

When Jonathan got a holiday job at Lonehead Flying Field, he expected a few enjoyable weeks of messing about with planes and a couple of flying lessons.
But when the sinister Mr Barrington-Ward appeared, Jon was suddenly launched into real airborne adventure – stolen planes, flying bullets and a cut-throat crew of political gangsters . . .

Operation Midnight 45p

It seemed as if it would never stop raining at Lonehead Flying Field. Then an urgent call from the Ministry of Defence plunged Jonathan and the rest of the team into a new adventure.
'Operation Midnight' – the code name for a mission to Africa to rescue Ephraim Demir from his border hideout. The mission became more and more dangerous as Jonathan found himself at the centre of a thrilling prison rescue . . .

Let Them All Starve 45p

Mambay is a poor country and when the rain stopped the people were dying like flies. Mrs Kidwallader-Jones was determined to help but the relief supplies were just not getting through.
So she hired Jonathan and his Lonehead Flying Field chums to fly out to Africa to find out why . . .

Roger Price

The Tomorrow People in **The Visitor** 40p

John, Stephen, Carol and Kenny – not just the ordinary kids they seem, but in fact The Tomorrow People – forerunners of a new race, *homo superior*. Gifted with superhuman powers, they have inter-galactic responsibility for the planet Earth. In this exciting adventure they track down an alien spaceship – and one false move could mean total destruction . . .

The Tomorrow People in **Three in Three** 30p

The professor who has the secret of total destruction . . . The Great Mothers of Matra, giant women who live for ever . . . The evil Guru Jedikiah, whose power matches that of the Tomorrow People themselves . . . Three exciting adventures which take the Tomorrow People from Scotland – to strange and distant planets – and back to California.

The Tomorrow People in **Four into Three** 40p

In this book the Tomorrow People are joined by Tyso, a young gypsy boy, in three more thrilling adventures in which they encounter the warlike Kraatans, whose one aim is to invade the Earth . . .
the Aliens, who appear suddenly in the lab and set the Tomorrow People against each other . . . and the villainous Kleptons, whose monstrous greed and cruelty brings them harsh punishment.

The Tomorrow People in **One Law** 35p

The Tomorrow People discover that there is another one of them, a young cockney called Mike. John, Stephen, Elizabeth and Tyso embark on another thrilling adventure as it appears that Mike is using his special powers to commit a crime . . .